Table of Contents

The Hollow Hills of Ireland

If you ever visit Ireland and walk in the green fields, you may see high round hills in the countryside. These hills may have thorn trees, the magic trees of the little people, on their tops. Old legends say that fairies, or Sidhe, as the Irish people call them, live in fairy palaces inside these magic hills.

Inside each hill, a king rules over hundreds of fairies. The king's palace is rich and beautiful, like the castles of human kings, but everything in it is magic. Since fairies do not work, they spend every day and night dancing, singing, and feasting on enchanted food. On summer nights a lucky traveler may see lights and hear beautiful music coming from the fairy hills. August 7, which is called Lammas Tide, is an especially good time to watch the hollow hills. On that night, the whole hill may rise up into the air while the fairies move to another hill along an invisible fairy road.

A wise person will not try to climb the magic hills, for the fairies pinch and poke people who trespass on their land. People who are foolish enough to try to dig up a hill to get the fairies' gold are in real danger. Many stories tell of how people digging into the hills are frightened away by strange voices, screams, and terrible storms. If the people come back and try again, such terrible accidents can happen to them that they sometimes die.

But people do sometimes see the palaces inside the hills. If someone is brave enough to walk around the hill nine times when the moon is full, the invisible door to the fairy palace will open and humans will be able to enter. The fairies themselves sometimes lure human musicians into the hills and make them stay to play for dances and feasts. But anyone who goes into a fairy hill must be very careful. The Sidhe will offer a visitor delicious-looking food which is really made of enchanted leaves and grass. Humans who eat any of this food are in the power of the fairies and become servants to the Sidhe forever. They can never leave the magic hill to return to the outside world.

Think About It
Would you be brave enough to enter the door of a fairy palace? Why or why not?

Sidhe is pronounced shē.

     2

Name _____

The Hollow Hills of Ireland

Main Idea
1. Choose another title for this story.

_____ Lammas Tide

_____ The Fairy King

_____ An Irish Legend

Sequencing
2. Number the events below in the order that they happened.

_____ The fairies lure human musicians inside.

_____ Humans who are not careful eat the food.

_____ The Sidhe offer visitors delicious-looking food.

_____ Humans become servants and can never leave.

Reading for Details
3. Scan the story and answer the questions.

Who are the Sidhe? _____

What do the Sidhe live in? _____

Where are the fairy palaces? _____

When is Lammas Tide? What is it? _____

_____

Why won't a wise person try to climb the magic hills? _____

_____

Reading for Understanding
Many things in my world are magic. Check the one that is not.

_____ trees

_____ hills

_____ gold

_____ palaces

_____ food

Since I do not have to work, I spend my time doing all of these things except

_____ dancing

_____ singing

_____ feasting

_____ sleeping

_____ pinching

When the Flowers Ran Away

Long ago, in Australia, there was once a time called Dreamtime, when spirits lived on the earth. People say the great spirit Baiame made the world and all the animals in it. He made the sky, the sun, the moon, and the stars. Baiame walked all over the earth and caused the rain to fall and the plants to grow. When he saw that the earth was green and beautiful and that the people were happy, he was content and knew that he could rest. So he made himself a home in the sky, which he called Pullima, where he could sit and look down at the prosperous earth.

Everything seemed to be perfect. But soon the flowers on earth grew dissatisfied, for they wanted to be with Baiame. So one night they softly climbed up to the sky and settled in Pullima, which became even brighter and more beautiful. When the people on earth woke in the morning, they looked for the flowers, but they were nowhere to be found. The people were so unhappy that they began to cry. The bees could not make honey, so they starved, and the butterflies had nowhere to rest.

Finally, some old men of the earth decided to try to find Baiame and ask for his help. They climbed for days up the side of a high mountain until they could see Baiame's home in the sky. And there were the flowers, as beautiful as ever. Baiame looked down and invited the old men to his home to rest and talk to him. The men pleaded with him to give back the flowers so the earth could be beautiful again. When he heard the men, Baiame was sad. He didn't want the earth people to be unhappy, but he didn't want his home to be without flowers.

Finally, Baiame told the men to pick as many flowers as they could carry. "These flowers," said Baiame, "will root and grow on earth. After the hottest days of summer have gone, the flowers will wither. Then they will be with me. But when spring comes again, I promise they will return." The men did as Baiame told them, and found that he had told the truth. The beautiful flowers grew on earth. Every year, at the end of summer, the flowers withered and died, but in the spring they came back again.

Think About It
Why do people like flowers so much?

Baiame is pronounced bä´yä mē.

Pullima is pronounced pul´lim uh.

Name _____

When the Flowers Ran Away

Main Idea

1. This story explains

_____ why there are spirits on earth.

_____ why flowers wither at the end of
summer and come back in the spring.

_____ why bees could not make honey.

Sequencing

2. Number the events below in the order that they happened.

_____ The people were unhappy without their flowers and asked Baiame for help.

_____ The flowers withered at the end of the summer.

_____ The men picked as many flowers as they could carry.

_____ The flowers grew dissatisfied on earth and went to Pullima.

_____ Baiame made the world and everything in it.

Reading for Details

3. Scan the story and answer the questions.

Who was Baiame? _____

What things did Baiame make? _____

Where did Baiame make his home? _____

Why did the flowers run away? _____

_____

When did the people notice the flowers were gone? _____

_____

Reading for Understanding

4. Write the correct letter in the space.

_____ Baiame   a. Baiame's home

_____ Pullima   b. Great Spirit

_____ wither   c. thriving and successful

_____ prosperous   d. to fade away and die

The Story of Babushka

Many years ago in old Russia, a poor old woman sat by the fire in her cottage one night. She lived all alone, for her husband was dead and her son was grown up, but she was not lonely. Her name was Babushka, and she had many happy memories.

It was winter, and snow was deep around the cottage. The wind howled, and it was bitter cold. Suddenly there was a knock at Babushka's door. She was surprised, because she thought no one would go out on such a terrible night. When she opened the door, she saw three men. They wore rich fur robes and gold rings, and they were strangers.

"May we come in?" they asked. Babushka invited them in, but she was ashamed that her house was so poor. "Don't be ashamed," they said. "We have come a long way, and we have a long way to go. We are looking for a great prince who has just been born in a far country. See, we have gifts for him. We have come to ask you to bring a gift and come with us."

Babushka did not know what to say. She had no gift for a prince, and she was too old for such a journey. "Please come with us," the strangers pleaded. "Please come and honor the new prince." But Babushka shook her head and said she was too old and too poor to go. So the men sadly went away.

When she was alone, the old woman couldn't forget the men's faces. They had wanted so much for her to go with them. Then she thought, "A baby wouldn't want gold. He would want toys to play with." So she hunted until she found a red ball and some wooden beads her son had played with long ago. She took the toys, put on her shawl, and went out into the night to find the three strangers.

"Wait for me," she called. But there was no answer. The men were gone. So Babushka traveled on and on looking for them, calling for them to wait for her. Some people say she is still searching for the three strangers and the prince. But wherever she goes, she stops to leave toys for good Russian children while they sleep.

Think About It
Why do you think Babushka leaves toys for children wherever she goes?

Babushka is pronounced bah boosh'kuh.

Name _____

The Story of Babushka

Main Idea

1. This story explains

_____ why Babushka searches for the strangers and the Prince.

_____ why some people take journeys.

_____ the Russian belief that children receive toys from an old woman while they sleep.

Sequencing

2. Number the events below in the order that they happened.

_____ The men invited Babushka on their journey.

_____ The strangers left without Babushka.

_____ Three strangers knocked on Babushka's door.

_____ Babushka searched for the strangers, leaving toys for good Russian children.

_____ Babushka found some toys for the Prince.

Reading for Details

3. Scan the story and answer the questions.

Where did Babushka live? _____

When did the strangers come to Babushka's door? _____

What did the strangers want? _____
_____

Why wouldn't Babushka go with them? _____
_____

Why did Babushka search for the strangers and the Prince? _____
_____

Reading for Understanding

4. Choose the best answer.

After the men left, Babushka felt

_____ regretful _____ forgetful _____ confused

Babushka went out into the night with toys because she was

_____ thoughtless _____ hopeful _____ crazy

Babushka continued looking for the men because she was

_____ dejected _____ distracted _____ determined

The Story of Kuma

The Ashanti people of Africa have a chief god named Nyamis. Nyamis has many children, called sons of heaven, who sometimes come down to the earth. People who are lucky enough to meet the gods should always listen to them and do just what they say. But one man, named Kuma, didn't listen, and this story tells what happened to him.

Kuma was a servant of the king of his people. He worked on the king's farm, and he always complained about how hard he worked. At night when he walked home, he complained about how poor he was. His neighbors never heard him do anything but complain. One day as he was walking down the road complaining, Kuma met a strange man.

"I am a son of heaven," said the man. "My father Nyamis sent me to look for you." The two men sat down in a big bowl with a chain around it. The people of heaven hauled them up by the chain until they came to a door. When the son of heaven opened the door, Kuma saw an old man sitting on a throne, dressed in rich robes of lion skin. Kuma knew that this was Nyamis.

"You are always complaining," Nyamis told Kuma. "I am getting tired of hearing you. It is not my fault that you are poor. Many people are poor all their lives. But now I am going to give you a present. Here are two sacks, a large one and a small one. The small one is for you, but you must give the large one to your king. Do not open your sack until you have given the king his present."

Kuma sat in the bowl again, and the people of heaven lowered him to earth. But when he got near the king's farm, Kuma had an idea. "Nobody knows that I have two sacks," he thought. "I will hide the big sack and give the small sack to the king." So he dug a hole and buried the big sack in a field. Then he went to see the king. When the king opened the small sack, it was filled with gold.

Kuma was very happy, for he remembered the large sack and thought of how rich he would be. He left the king's house and ran as fast as he could to dig up the sack. With trembling fingers he untied the sack, tipped it over, and out poured – stones!

Think About It
What do you think Kuma did after he found stones in the large sack?

Kuma is pronounced koo'muh.

Ashanti is pronounced ä shän'tē.

Nyamis is pronounced ny'ah mis.

Name _____

The Story of Kuma

Main Idea

1. This story tells about

_____ a man who took a ride in a big bowl.

_____ a man who was greedy.

_____ a man who was a servant of the king.

Sequencing

2. Number the events below in the order that they happened.

_____ Kuma was walking down the road complaining.

_____ Nyamis gave Kuma two sacks.

_____ Kuma untied the big sack and found stones.

_____ Kuma was taken to see Nyamis.

_____ Kuma gave the small sack to the king.

Reading for Details

3. Scan the story and answer the questions.

Who has a chief god named Nyamis? _____

What was Kuma always complaining about? _____

_____

Where did Kuma meet the son of heaven? _____

When was Kuma supposed to open the small sack? _____

_____

Why did Kuma think he could give the small sack to the king?_____

_____

Reading for Understanding

4. When an author tells what a character says, thinks, feels, or does, it helps you get to know the character. Check the things you learned about Kuma.

_____ He was a complainer.

_____ He was happy.

_____ He was a cheater.

_____ He was greedy.

_____ He was a good listener.

Theseus and the Minotaur

In ancient Greece, there once lived a ferocious beast, called the Minotaur, who had the head of a bull and the body of a man. The Minotaur lived on the island of Crete, in the center of a twisting maze called the Labyrinth. Anyone entering the Labyrinth became hopelessly lost and wandered until the Minotaur found him and ate him. At that time, Crete was ruled by cruel and powerful King Minos. Every year, King Minos would go to the nearby city of Athens and demand seven maidens and seven youths to feed to the Minotaur. If the Athenians refused to give up the young people, King Minos threatened to destroy the city.

One year, the mighty hero Theseus happened to come to Athens. He was strong and fearless, and he loved danger. So he offered to be one of the Minotaur's victims. The Athenians gratefully accepted, for they hoped that he could defeat the Minotaur and free the city at last.

The fourteen young people were brought to Crete and shown to the Cretans before being sent to the Labyrinth. There King Minos' daughter, Ariadne, saw Theseus and fell in love with him. She wanted to save him, so she asked Daedelus, the man who had made the Labyrinth, for help. Then she went to Theseus in prison and told him she would help him if he promised to marry her. He agreed, and she told him of Daedelus' plan.

The next day, Theseus took a ball of thread with him when he was thrown into the Labyrinth. As he walked, he unwound the thread behind him. Then he went looking for the Minotaur and beat it with his fists. The struggle seemed to last forever, but at last the Minotaur fell dead. Theseus had triumphed. Then, by following the thread back to the entrance, he brought the other thirteen people to safety.

Ariadne was very happy to see Theseus was safe. And the people of Athens joyfully celebrated the great defeat of the terrible Minotaur.

Think About It

Have you ever had a hero? Who was it and why?

Theseus is pronounced thee´soos.

Minotaur is pronounced min´uh tawr.

Ariadne is pronounced ar i ad´nē.

Daedelus is pronounced ded´ uh lus.

Minos is pronounced mī´ nos.

Theseus and the Minotaur

Main Idea

1. This story tells

_____ how Ariadne fell in love with Theseus.

_____ how Theseus freed Athens from the Minotaur.

_____ how fourteen young people came to Crete.

Sequencing

2. Number the events below in the order that they happened.

_____ The people of Athens celebrated.

_____ Theseus offered to be King Minos' victim.

_____ Theseus defeated the Minotaur.

_____ Fourteen young people escaped from the Labyrinth.

_____ Ariadne fell in love with Theseus and offered to help him.

Reading for Details

3. Scan the story and answer the questions.

Where did this story take place? _____

When did King Minos go to Athens? _____

Why did he go ? _____

_____

Why did Theseus take a ball of thread with him into the Labyrinth? _____

_____

Who celebrated the defeat of the Minotaur? _____

Reading for Understanding

4. Write the correct letter in the space.

_____ Minotaur   a. ruler of Crete

_____ Labyrinth   b. city in ancient Greece

_____ King Minos   c. maker of the Labyrinth

_____ Crete   d. beast

_____ Athens   e. maze

_____ Theseus   f. island in the center of the Labyrinth

_____ Ariadne   g. daughter of King Minos

_____ Daedelus   h. hero

Beowulf, the Mighty Hero

There once was a king in England named Hrothgar, who had won many battles against his enemies. He had rooms full of treasure and hundreds of loyal soldiers to protect him. But besides being rich, he was wise and kind, and his people were happy. Hrothgar loved to give feasts for his friends and warriors, and for miles around people could hear the music and laughter from Hrothgar's great hall. Life seemed perfect for the king and the people of England.

But deep in the nearby swamp, the monster Grendel was not happy. He hated Hrothgar, and even more, he hated the happy sounds coming from the great hall. So one night he left his cave in the swamp, and crept into the great hall where Hrothgar's soldiers lay sleeping. When Hrothgar came down from his chamber the next morning, he found nearly all of his men dead. Hrothgar was furious that the monster had killed his friends, and he wanted revenge. But he could not fight Grendel by himself and most of his soldiers were dead. There was not a hero left in all England to fight for him.

Across the sea in Denmark, a great hero named Beowulf heard about Grendel's terrible deed. He knew Hrothgar was a good king, so he went to him and suggested a plan to kill the monster. That night, Beowulf set a trap for Grendel. He put his soliders in the hall, and pretended to have a feast. When Grendel heard the noise, he stormed to the castle, determined to kill all those within.

But as Grendel entered the castle, Beowulf jumped out at him. Grendel roared at the trick, and lunged at Beowulf. The two fought so fiercely that they nearly destroyed the castle. Grendel seemed to be winning until Beowulf ripped Grendel's arm off. Grendel cried out in pain, and with his good arm, threw Beowulf to the ground. Before Beowulf could get back on his feet, Grendel ran back to his cave. Beowulf chased the monster, but by the time he got to Grendel's cave, the monster lay dead.

Hrothgar and his people were saved! And to honor their new hero, many long and happy feasts were held in the castle.

Think About It
How do you think Beowulf felt after he saved Hrothgar and his people?

Beowulf is pronounced bay'uh wulf.

Hrothgar is pronounced hroth'gär.

Name _____

Beowulf, the Mighty Hero

Main Idea

1. This story tells how

_____ Beowulf saved Hrothgar and his people.

_____ Grendel killed the soldiers.

_____ perfect life was in England.

Sequencing

2. Number the events below in the order that they happened.

_____ Grendel killed many of Hrothgar's soldiers.

_____ Grendel fought Beowulf.

_____ Beowulf found Grendel dead.

_____ Beowulf set a trap for Grendel.

_____ Beowulf heard about Grendel's terrible deed.

Reading for Details

3. Scan the story and answer the questions.

Who was Hrothgar? _____

What did Hrothgar love to do? _____

_____

Where did Grendel live? _____

When did Hrothgar find most of his men dead? _____

_____

Why did Beowulf go to Hrothgar? _____

_____

Reading for Understanding

4. Circle yes or no.

I could have caught Grendel.	Yes	No
If Hrothgar gets into trouble again, I will save him.	Yes	No
If Hrothgar invites me to another feast, I will go.	Yes	No

Pyole and Krishna

The Hindu children of India know that the gods are always close by. If a child asks for help, sometimes a god will answer the call. This story is about a poor boy who needed help and how Krishna, a great god, answered him.

Pyole was a small boy who lived alone with his mother in a small village in India. Though they were very poor, Pyole's mother wanted him to go to school. But the nearest school was in a village on the other side of the forest. Pyole had no money to live at the school like the other children, so every day he walked through the forest to school and back again.

The forest was huge and frightening. Wild animals hid behind rocks and snakes hung from the branches. In the morning the sun lit the path, but in the evening when Pyole returned home from school, the tall trees made the path very dark. Every evening Pyole became more and more afraid of the voices of the animals and the eyes that shone at him from the darkness. Finally he refused to go to school.

"Call to Lord Krishna when you are frightened by the dark," Pyole's mother told him. "He will go with you through the forest."

The next evening when he entered the dark forest, Pyole remembered his mother's words. He called out to Krishna to walk with him. At once, the bushes rustled, and a tall man in a simple robe walked toward Pyole. His face was so kind that Pyole held out his hand to the stranger. As they crossed the forest, the man played on a flute that was hung around his neck, and a blue light shone all around. At the edge of the forest, Krishna left Pyole. And every evening, the god walked through the forest with the boy.

Soon Pyole's teacher heard about the stranger walking through the forest and asked if he could come and see the great god too. So one day Pyole took the teacher into the forest and called on Krishna to walk with them. But Krishna did not come. Instead, a blue light shone, and a voice said, "I am only seen by people who need me to guide them. Your teacher is a great man and does not need to see me." But the blue light still lit the path homeward as Pyole and the teacher walked through the forest.

Think About It
When you are frightened by something, what do you do to help yourself feel safe again?

Pyole is pronounced pī'ō lē.

Krishna is pronounced krish'nuh.

14

Pyole and Krishna

Main Idea

1. Choose another title for this story.

_____ How a Call for Help was Answered

_____ A Frightening Forest

_____ A Blue Light

Sequencing

2. Number the events below in the order that they happened.

_____ Kirshna walked through the forest with Pyole.

_____ His mother told Pyole to call on the god, Krishna, to walk through the forest with him.

_____ Pyole walked to school everyday through a huge and frightening forest.

_____ Pyole refused to go to school.

_____ Krishna refused to appear before Pyole's teacher.

Reading for Details

3. Scan the story and answer the questions.

Who knows that the gods are always close by? _____

_____

What hides behind the rocks in the forest? _____

_____

Where was the nearest school? _____

_____

When did Krishna walk through the forest with Pyole? _____

_____

Why didn't Krishna let Pyole's teacher see him? _____

_____

Reading for Understanding

4. Place the descriptive word or phrase in the correct column.

huge and frightening, tall, wild animals and snakes, in a
simple robe, tall trees, kind face, played a flute, very dark,
animal voices and shining eyes, surrounded by blue light

Forest	Krishna
_____	_____
_____	_____
_____	_____
_____	_____
_____	_____
_____	_____

The Greatest Oil Man

About a hundred years ago, people came from all around the country to drill for oil in east Texas. The oil drillers were tough men, and the only things meaner than the men were the Texas sandstorms. Every oil driller loved to brag about how strong and smart he was. But they all agreed that the greatest oil man of all was Kemp Morgan.

Nobody really knew Morgan very well because he worked alone and never stayed in one place for long. Usually it took a big gang of men to find oil and dig a well. But Morgan could do the whole thing by himself. First, he would walk around the sandy country sniffing. His nose was so good, he could smell the oil under the ground. When he found oil, he would pick up his shovel. Most people used a drill, but Morgan just dug with his shovel until he hit hard rock. Then he would put up a derrick, the tall tower that holds the drill, all by himself, and begin drilling. Once he started the engine on his drill, he would keep going twenty-four hours a day until he struck oil. Then he would move on, looking for more oil.

Morgan was so strong that sometimes he drilled too deep. People say that once, instead of hitting oil, he hit a rubber mine in Brazil. Pure rubber came out of the drill hole. Morgan didn't care, though. He cut off ten-foot pieces and sold them to tire factories in Ohio.

Another time, Morgan was looking for oil when his nose told him a sandstorm was coming. So he tied his mules to some trees and sat down to wait for the storm to pass. The wind howled all night long. He rolled up in his blanket and went to sleep. When he woke up, his mules were gone. He couldn't find them anywhere until he looked up. The sandstorm had been so fierce that it had blown the sand away from under the mules. They were hanging from trees thirty feet in the air! But Morgan just bent the trees down, cut the mules loose, and went on his way.

Even though he was the greatest of the oil men, Kemp Morgan was modest. He didn't brag. In fact, he didn't talk much at all. He just kept moving along and drilling new wells. Some say that all the oil wells in Texas and Oklahoma were started by Kemp Morgan.

Think About It
This story is called a tall tale. That means it is **exaggerated**. What parts of the story are exaggerated?

Name _____

The Greatest Oil Man

Main Idea

1. Choose another title for this story.

_____ How to Start an Oil Well

_____ A Texas Sandstorm

_____ A Tale about Kemp Morgan

Sequencing

2. Number the events below in order.

_____ He would dig with a shovel until he hit hard rock.

_____ Morgan would move on looking for more oil.

_____ Morgan would put up a derrick.

_____ Morgan would smell oil in the ground.

_____ He would drill for twenty-four hours a day until he struck oil.

Reading for Details

3. Scan the story and answer the questions.

Who thought that Kemp Morgan was the greatest oil man of all?_____

_____

What did Morgan sell to tire factories in Ohio? _____

_____

When did Morgan discover that his mules were missing? _____

_____

Where did Morgan find his mules after the sandstorm?_____

_____

Why didn't people know Kemp Morgan very well ? _____

_____

Reading for Understanding

4. Even though I don't talk much, people talk a lot about me.

Check the one thing they do not say about me.

_____ I work alone.

_____ I can put up a derrick all by myself.

_____ I run a drill twenty-four hours a day.

_____ I sometimes fall asleep while I'm drilling and then drill too deep.

_____ I move around a lot.

The Singing Birds

A long time ago, according to American Indian legend, the Great Spirit made the world. He made the land and the sky, the lakes and the rivers. Then, to make the world green and beautiful, he made trees and flowers, and he put the reed beside the lakes. But the Great Spirit was lonely, so he made many different animals. Some that he made lived in the forests, and some lived on the prairies or in the oceans. Soon the whole world was full of animals. Still the Great Spirit was not finished. He made the water birds to swim on the lakes and wade in the marshes. But he didn't make any small birds, and none of the birds could sing.

When the first cold days came, the leaves on the trees turned yellow and brown and fell from the branches. The animals hid away in holes and burrows. Some of them went to sleep, and without the animals, the whole world became very still. The Great Spirit listened. But all he could hear was the lonely wind and the sound of the water on the shore. The silence made him sad, and he wished for the warm days to come again.

Then as he watched the last leaves fall from a tall tree, the Great Spirit had an idea. He stretched out his hand. The leaves did not fall to the ground but instead became little birds. They were the colors of the leaves, yellow and red and brown. The Great Spirit smiled when he saw the tiny colorful birds flying through the bare trees. Now he would not be lonely, for the birds would stay with him all through the winter.

As he watched the little birds fly, the Great Spirit thought about what he would do when the warm days came. "I shall teach them to build nests in the trees and grasses. When their eggs hatch, I will help them care for their fledglings. Then there will be more little birds to stay with me in the winter."

But still the Great Spirit was not completely happy. The birds were with him, but the world was still silent. Suddenly the Great Spirit put out his hand again. At once every bird had a voice. They called to each other about the warm days to come, and the world was not silent any more. The Great Spirit was happy at last.

Think About It
Imagine living in a silent world. What five things would you miss hearing? Why?

18

The Singing Birds

Main Idea

1. This story is an Indian legend that explains

_____ how the Great Spirit made many different animals.

_____ why the Great Spirit was lonely in the winter.

_____ why the Great Spirit gave a voice to every bird.

Sequencing

2. Number the events below in the order that they happened.

_____ The Great Spirit made the world.

_____ The Great Spirit changed the falling leaves into birds.

_____ Because he was lonely, the Great Spirit made many animals.

_____ The birds stayed with the Great Spirit all winter.

_____ The animals hid away in the winter.

_____ The Great Spirit gave a voice to every bird.

Reading for Details

3. Scan the story and answer the questions.

Who told this story? _____

What colors were the birds? _____

Where did the animals hide? _____

When did the Great Spirit smile? _____

Why did the Great Spirit make the little birds? _____

_____

Reading for Understanding

4. Circle Yes or No.

When all I could hear was the wind and the water, I was happy.	Yes	No
When I made the birds, I knew that I would no longer be lonely in the winter.	Yes	No
Even though the birds could not sing, I was completely happy.	Yes	No
When every bird had a voice, I was happy.	Yes	No

John Henry, the Steel Driving Man

The legend of John Henry comes to us from the southern United States. John Henry was a hero of the people who worked the fields and built the railroads, for John Henry was the biggest and strongest working man of all. People still talk about his famous battle against the steam drill and about how he could swing his hammer harder and faster than anyone else in the world.

John Henry was born a slave in Virginia and worked hard picking cotton and plowing fields. When he was freed after the American Civil War, he got a job building the Big Bend Railroad Tunnel for the Chesapeake and Ohio Railroad. Building tunnels in those days was hard work. Men had to dig through mountains, breaking rock with hammers whose heads weighed twelve pounds. John Henry was such a big and strong man that he had a special hammer made with a sixteen pound head! Often people for miles around could see the sparks fly as John Henry drove his hammer into the rock.

Then one day, a man showed up at the tunnel with a steam-powered drill for sale. John Henry's boss didn't think he needed to buy that drill because he knew how good John Henry was. But the salesman said, "If any man can outwork my steam drill, you can have it for free!" "Nothing can beat John Henry!" cried the men, and the contest began.

At first, the drill took the lead, but John Henry said, "Don't worry. I'm just loosening up." Then his muscles got loose, and John Henry pulled ahead. He worked and worked, driving through the mountain. Fire came from his hammer, and he had to ask the water boy to throw a bucket of water on it. For hours, the steam drill and John Henry battled each other. The workmen cheered their hero on as rock flew into the air.

At last, time was up. The steam drill had drilled through nine feet of rock, but John Henry had drilled through sixteen feet! John Henry had beat the steam drill! But as he did, he laid down his hammer and died. But even today, people in Virginia say that early in the morning, you can still hear John Henry's hammer ring.

Think About It
Do you think that John Henry was a real man? Why or why not?

Name _____

John Henry, the Steel Driving Man

Main Idea

1. Choose another title for this story.

_____ The Contest

_____ The Legend of John Henry

_____ Steam Drill for Sale

Sequencing

2. Number the events below in the order that they happened.

_____ John Henry had drilled through sixteen feet of rock.

_____ A man showed up at the tunnel with a steam-powered drill for sale.

_____ John Henry got a job building railroad tunnels.

_____ John Henry was born a slave in Virginia.

Reading for Details

3. Scan the story to answer these questions.

Who was born a slave? _____

Where was John Henry born? _____

What did John Henry do as a slave? _____

When was John Henry freed? _____

Why did John Henry's boss think he didn't need the steam-powered drill? _____

_____

Reading for Understanding

4. Circle yes or no.

People say that I am the biggest and scariest working man of all.	Yes	No
People say that I can swing my hammer higher and faster than anyone else.	Yes	No
People come from far away to watch me drive my sixteen pound hammer head into the rock.	Yes	No
People say that they can still hear my hammer ring early in the morning.	Yes	No

The Building of the Round Table

Stories have been told about King Arthur and his knights for more than a thousand years. According to the legends, Arthur and his court lived in the magic city of Camelot in England. The city was as beautiful as Arthur was wise and good, and the brave knights who lived in Arthur's palace protected the weak and fought evil. And one of the most wonderful things in Arthur's great court was the famous Round Table.

Before the Round Table was built, Arthur had a great long table that stood in the middle of the Great Hall. A fine chair was set at the table for every knight and his lady, and each seat was carved and trimmed with gold. Most knights were perfectly happy to take any seat at all, but a few knights insisted that they should have seats at the head of the table. The trouble spread, and one night at dinner quarrels broke out among the knights. Each began to argue that he was braver and nobler than the others and so deserved the first seat at the table. Soon the quarrels became fights. Plates began to fly as the knights threw them at each other. The crashing dishes and barking dogs made a terrible racket. Knights drew their swords and began to duel. Arthur had had enough! He jumped to his feet and declared that anyone who fought would be put to death.

But Arthur knew that he needed a better way to stop the fighting. Suddenly there was a knock on the castle door, and an old man entered. He wore common workmen's clothes and carried tools. "I know how to solve your problem," he said. And as Arthur and his knights watched, the strange man set about building a round table. Arthur's problem was solved! The table was big enough to seat all the knights, yet light enough to be carried along when the king went to war. And since a round table has no head, no matter where the knights sat, they were always equal.

The old man would take no money for his work and quietly disappeared into the night, never to be seen again. But thanks to his wonderful round table, peace returned to Camelot.

Think About It
Who do you think the old man was? Where do you think he went?

Name _____

The Building of
the Round Table

Main Idea
1. Choose another title for this story.

_____ A New Table for King Arthur's Knights

_____ King Arthur and his Knights

_____ A Mystery Man

Sequencing
2. Number the events below in the order that they happened.

_____ The old man built a round table.

_____ A quarrel broke out among the knights.

_____ The knights sat around the table as equals.

_____ King Arthur declared that anyone who fought would be put to death.

_____ Soon the quarrel became a fight.

Reading for Details
3. Scan the story to answer these questions.

Where did King Arthur and his knights live? _____

What stood in the middle of the Great Hall of Arthur's castle? _____

Why did that table cause trouble? _____

Who helped solve the problem in Camelot? _____

When did peace return to Camelot? _____

_____

Reading for Understanding
4. Put each descriptive word in the correct column. Not all the words will be used.

magic, wise, brave, strange, beautiful, good, noble, common, round, long

Camelot	King Arthur	Knights
_____	_____	_____
_____	_____	_____
_____	_____	_____

Bellerophon and Pegasus

Pegasus was the winged horse of Greek mythology. He sprang full-grown from the blood of a monster killed by the great hero Perseus. Pegasus would allow no one to own or ride him, and he would quickly fly away whenever a human came near.

Bellerophon, a noble young Greek man, saw Pegasus and immediately wanted to own him. But he did not know how to capture the winged horse. Then, a wise man named Polydius told Bellerophon to go and sleep at the temple of the Goddess Athena. There, in a dream, Bellerophon saw the goddess holding out a golden bridle. When he awoke, he found the bridle lying on the floor beside him.

Bellerophon took the magic bridle and went to look for Pegasus. When he found the horse grazing in a field, Bellerophon crept up and quickly slipped the bridle over Pegasus' head. Pegasus did not fight Bellerophon, but let the youth get on his back and ride him. The two of them became great friends and traveled all over the world together, looking for excitement.

Among the many adventures Bellerophon and Pegasus had was a battle with the Chimaera. This huge beast had the body of a goat, the head of a lion, and the tail of a snake. No one, it seemed, could get close enough to kill the awful creature, for it breathed fire, killing anyone who tried to fight it. But Bellerophon rode Pegasus into the sky just beyond the monster's reach and shot it with a mighty bow and arrow. Thus, they earned the gratitude of the people in the land where the Chimaera had lived.

Bellerophon lived happily with Pegasus for some time. Then he began to think himself great enough to live with the gods themselves. So he tried to ride Pegasus to Mount Olympus, the home of the gods. But Pegasus knew that Bellerophon could never enter Olympus and sadly threw him off his back. Bellerophon lived a lonely, unhappy life separated from his companion. Pegasus, however, went to Olympus and lived in the golden stalls of the gods' horses. Forever afterwards, he served Zeus, the greatest of the gods.

Think About It
Have you ever had a pet that was your special friend? Tell or write about it.

Polydius is pronounced pŏ li'dēus.

Bellerophon is pronounced be ler'o fon.

Pegasus is pronounced peg'a sus.

Perseus is pronounced pĕr'sus.

Athena is pronounced a thē'na.

Chimaera is pronounced chi mae'ra.

24

Name _____

Bellerophon and Pegasus

Main Idea

1. This story explains

_____ the friendship of Pegasus and Bellerophon.

_____ Bellerophon's dream.

_____ the battle with the Chimaera.

Sequencing

2. Number the events below in the order that they happened.

_____ Bellerophon and Pegasus had a battle with the Chimaera.

_____ Bellerophon tried to ride Pegasus to Mount Olympus.

_____ Bellerophon and Pegasus became great friends.

_____ Pegasus served Zeus forever afterwards.

_____ Pegasus sadly threw Bellerophon off his back.

Reading for Details

3. Scan the story to answer these questions.

Who was the only person able to capture Pegasus? _____

What did Bellerophon use to capture Pegasus? _____

When did Bellerophon find the bridle? _____

_____

Where did Bellerophon and Pegasus travel together? _____

_____

Why did Pegasus throw Bellerophon off his back? _____

_____

Reading for Understanding

4. Place the correct letter in the blank.

_____ Pegasus   a. young Greek man

_____ Bellerophon   b. god

_____ Polydius   c. winged horse

_____ Athena   d. wise man

_____ Chimaera   e. goddess

_____ Mt. Olympus   f. beast

_____ Zeus   g. home of the gods

The Extra Days of the Year

The most powerful and most loved of all the ancient Egyptian gods was Ra. For many years he ruled the people of Egypt wisely and kindly. But one day he learned something that brought him great sorrow. Ra could see into the future, and he foresaw that his daughter, Nut, would one day have a child who would destroy Ra's body. To prevent this tragedy, Ra put a curse on his daughter, saying that she would bear no child on any day of the year.

But Nut loved children and longed to have a child of her own. So she asked her brother Thoth to help her. Wise Thoth soon thought of a plan to help his sister. He went to see Konsu, the Moon-god, and challenged him to a game of checkers. Now, Konsu had one weakness–he couldn't resist playing games of skill. So he not only accepted Thoth's challenge, but bet some of his moonlight that he would win. They played one game after another, but Thoth, the wisest of all Ra's children, won every game. At the end of five games, Thoth had won enough moonlight from Konsu to make five extra days. And poor Konsu had lost so much of his light that to this day the moon's light wanes for a few days each month.

The five extra days Thoth had won were put between the end of the old year and the beginning of the new year and became holidays. So instead of the year having 360 days as before, it now had 365. And, over the years, each of Nut's five children was born on one of these holidays. Ra's curse had worked, for Nut bore no children on any day of the year. But because of the extra days Thoth had won from Konsu, Nut was able to have children in spite of Ra's curse.

The future that Ra had foreseen at last came true. One of Nut's children, Osiris, did destroy the body of Ra, and the great god was forced to leave the earth. But Ra became the sun-god and so was still able to help his people. Every day he traveled across the sky, bringing light and warmth to Egypt. And at night Ra carried the souls of the dead to the underworld in his glorious golden boat.

Think About It
Make up a myth to explain why there is summer or winter.

Thoth is pronounced tōt.

Konsu is pronounced kän'sü.

Name _____

The Extra Days
of the Year

Main Idea
1. Long ago people made up myths to explain why things happened. This myth explains

_____ why Ra became the sun-god.

_____ why Nut could not have any children.

_____ why a year has 365 days and the moon grows smaller every month.

Sequencing
2. Number the events below in the order that they happened.

_____ Thoth challenged Konsu to a game of checkers.

_____ Thoth won enough moonlight to make five extra days.

_____ Ra put a curse on Nut.

_____ Nut had five children.

_____ Nut asked Thoth for help.

Reading for Details
3. Scan the story to answer these questions.

Who was Ra? _____

What was the curse that Ra put on Nut? _____

_____

Where did Thoth put the five extra days? _____

_____

When did Nut have her children? _____

Why was Ra forced to leave the earth? _____

_____

Reading for Understanding
4. Place the correct letter in the blank.

_____ Ra   a. Nut's brother

_____ Nut   b. Nut's child

_____ Thoth   c. Sun-god

_____ Konsu   d. Moon-god

_____ Osirus   e. Ra's daughter

Li Ching and the Rain Makers

According to Chinese legend, dragon-gods made the sky, the earth, and all the people and animals. The dragon-gods lived in splendid homes beyond the sky, where they were responsible for making rain. In this way, the dragon-gods were supposed to take care of the people on earth, but sometimes they needed help.

One day, a great scholar named Li Ching was hunting in the forest when he spotted a deer. Although he chased it for hours, it escaped him, and he found himself in a strange land. Night was coming, and Li Ching was lost. Through the rising mist he saw lights and followed them to a grand palace. His knock on the door was answered by a beautifully dressed woman. She took pity on Li Ching and said he could spend the night.

Li Ching had only been asleep for a few hours when someone woke him up. "You must help me," cried the woman. "My sons are the dragon rain makers. Tonight they were supposed to ride through the sky to make rain, but they cannot return from their travels in time to do so. Our masters will be displeased if there is no rain, for there has been a great drought." She gave Li Ching her sons' magic horse and a small jar. Li Ching was instructed to put one drop of water from the jar on the horse's mane at every cloud.

Li Ching mounted the horse, and it leaped into the air. At every cloud the horse stopped, and Li Ching shook one drop of water onto the horse's mane. The horse tossed its head, and the drop fell to the cloud below. All night they rode, stopping at every cloud, and in the morning they returned to the palace.

The mother of the dragon rain makers was waiting for Li Ching at the gate. "Thank you so much for helping," she said, as she handed him a small silk bag filled with pearls. Then she showed him a path that would lead him back to his village and bid him farewell. As Li Ching looked back, the lady and the palace vanished in the mist.

When Li Ching arrived home, his friends ran to meet him, talking of the great rain that had ended the long drought. Li Ching smiled, but said nothing.

Think About It
Why didn't Li Ching tell his friends what he had done?

Name _____

Li Ching and the Rain Makers

Main Idea
1. This story explains

_____ how the dragon rain makers could not make rain.

_____ how Li Ching helped make the rain that ended the long drought.

_____ how Li Ching lost his way.

Sequencing
2. Number the events below in the order that they happened.

_____ Li Ching rode the horse all night long making the rain.

_____ His friends ran to meet him and told him about the great rain.

_____ Li Ching went hunting and got lost.

_____ Li Ching was given a bag of pearls for his help and shown the way home.

_____ He found a grand palace.

Reading for Details
3. Scan the story to answer these questions.

Who tells the legend about the dragon gods?_____

What did the woman ask Li Ching to do? _____

Where was Li Ching instructed to put the drop of water? _____

_____

When did Li Ching return to the palace? _____

Why didn't the woman's sons make the rain? _____

_____

Reading for Understanding
4. Place the letter in the correct blank.

_____ Li Ching   a. made the sky, earth, people, and animals

_____ Dragon-gods   b. no rainfall for a long time

_____ drought   c. a great scholar

_____ vanish   d. to disappear

The Flying Dutchman

Sailors tell many stories of the mysteries of the sea, of lost ships and ghost crews. But one of the strangest of the sea stories is the tale of The Flying Dutchman. The very name of this ill-fated ship freezes the hearts of sailors who must take their ships around the Cape of Good Hope, the southern tip of Africa.

Many years ago a Dutch ship was sailing home from the rich islands beyond India. The ship was loaded with silk and spices to be sold back in the Netherlands. The only passenger on board was a Dutchman who had lived for many years in the East Indies. He had made a great deal of money and was now going back to the Netherlands to spend his final years in peace. The captain, too, was going home, never to sail again. He had with him on board all the money he had saved in many years of sailing. As the ship neared the Cape of Good Hope, these two men began talking about how they would spend all their money when they reached home.

While the two talked, one of the crew listened outside the door. This evil man began planning to take the gold. He gathered the rest of the crew, and together they broke in and seized the Dutchman and the captain. After finding their money, the crew tied the two poor men up and threw them into the sea.

Delighted with their new riches, the crew set sail for the nearest port so they could spend their stolen gold. But a mysterious plague suddenly broke out among the crew, making them crave water to cool their burning throats. Then, as they neared a city where they could get water, a sudden storm came up and blew the ship away from the shore. Again they tried to reach port, and again a storm blew them far out to sea. Every time the ship neared a port, it was driven back by a fierce gale.

Some say The Flying Dutchman and its ghostly crew still sail the sea near the Cape of Good Hope, trying desperately to reach land. And since the legend says that the ghost ship bodes disaster for the unlucky person who sees it, sailors near the Cape of Good Hope keep their fingers crossed and hope The Flying Dutchman never comes looming out of the fog toward them.

Think About It
Why do you think the plague broke out on the ship?

The Flying Dutchman

Main Idea

1. This story tells

_____ about a robbery at sea.

_____ why a ghost ship sails near the Cape of Good Hope.

_____ about a rich Dutchman.

Sequencing

2. Number the events below in the order that they happened.

_____ The captain and the rich passenger talked about their riches.

_____ The ship tried unsuccessfully to reach the shore.

_____ The Flying Dutchman was sailing back to the Netherlands.

_____ The crew tied up the captain and the passenger and threw them overboard.

_____ A mysterious plague broke out among the crew.

Reading for Details

3. Scan the story to answer these questions.

Who tells the sea stories? _____

What is the Flying Dutchman? _____

_____

Where was the ship sailing to? _____

When did the crew tie up the captain and the passenger and throw them overboard? _____

_____

Why do sailors near the Cape of Good Hope keep their fingers crossed? _____

Reading for Understanding

4. Circle yes or no.

I say that the Flying Dutchman is still haunting the Cape of Good Hope.	Yes	No
My story begins when the ship was sailing back to the islands off India.	Yes	No
After we got rid of the captain and the passenger, we headed for the nearest port.	Yes	No
I got sick and was very thirsty, but I saw a doctor when I reached port.	Yes	No

31

How Cuchulainn Got his Name

Cuchulainn was one of the greatest heroes in the legends of ancient Ireland. He was as strong as the Greek hero, Hercules, and he led his king's army to many victories against its enemies. But Cuchulainn was not always known by that name. Like many other heroes, he was given a different name at birth. Cuchulainn, his hero name, was given in honor of his first famous deed.

When Cuchulainn was born, his mother was told by a god that her baby would become a great hero. So she took him to Concobar, the Irish king, to be raised among the finest warriors in the land. King Concobar called the boy Setanta, and all the king's people wanted to help raise this strong, handsome baby.

As Setanta grew, he became the strongest of all the boys at the king's palace. By the time he was ten years old, Setanta was the best at all sports and could win a wrestling match against a man twice his size. One day, when Setanta was playing ball in the courtyard, King Concobar asked him to go to a banquet being given by Culann, the king's blacksmith and friend. Setanta told the king to go on, saying that he would follow when his game was done.

When the king and his warriors arrived at Culann's house, the smith, as was his custom, set his watchdog loose in the yard to guard the house. But this was no ordinary dog. It stood as tall as a cow and was fiercer than a hundred hounds.

Unfortunately, everyone had forgotton that Setanta was coming. When he arrived, the dog rushed at him to tear him to pieces. Setanta, however, was fearless. Just as the terrible dog was about to leap at his throat, Setanta stuffed the ball he was carrying into the dog's mouth. Then he lifted the great dog over his head and smashed it on a rock.

Culann was angry at Setanta for killing his dog, and demanded payment, so Setanta promised to find and train another dog. But Culann had no dog to guard his house in the meantime. So Setanta promised to guard the house himself, like a watchdog, until the new dog was trained. And ever after he was called Cuchulainn, which means "Culann's hound," in memory of his first adventure.

Think About It
Do you think Cuchulainn chose the best solution to his problem? Why or why not?

Cuchulainn is pronounced kö chö'lān.

Culann is pronounced kö'lan.

How Cuchulainn Got his Name

Main Idea

1. Choose another title for this story.

_____ A New Name for Setanta

_____ Cuchulainn's First Adventure

_____ An Unusual Watchdog

Sequencing

2. Number the events below in the order that they happened.

_____ Setanta arrived at Culann's house later.

_____ Setanta promised to guard the house until a new dog was trained.

_____ Setanta killed Culann's hound.

_____ The king arrived first at Culann's house.

_____ The king asked Setanta to go to a banquet at the blacksmith's house.

_____ Setanta was given the name Cuchulainn.

Reading for Details

3. Scan the story to answer these questions.

Where did this story take place? _____

Who told Setanta's mother that her baby would become a great hero?_____

_____

What was special about Setanta as he was growing? _____

_____

When did Culann let his dog out into the yard? _____

_____

Why was Culann angry with Setanta? _____

Reading for Understanding

4. Choose another solution to each of Setanta's problems.

When the dog rushed at Setanta, he could have

_____ stuffed the ball into the dog's mouth and then ran into the house.

_____ ran up a tree.

_____ thrown the ball and played a game with the dog.

When Culann was angry at Setanta and demanded payment, Setanta could have

_____ given him money to buy and train a new dog.

_____ told him that he was simply defending himself and owed him nothing.

_____ borrowed another dog.

Atalanta and the Golden Apples

Many legends have come down to us from ancient Greece, but one of the best is about the remarkable Atalanta, a woman who was beautiful, strong, and fleet of foot.

When Atalanta was born, her father was disappointed, for he had wanted a son. So he took his daughter to a mountainside and left her to die. But Atalanta was discovered by a bear who nursed her and raised her. Later, kindly hunters adopted her and taught her the ways of humans.

As Atalanta grew, she became a strong fighter and a fast runner. In fact, she could run faster than any of the young men she met and could out-wrestle them as well. Because she was beautiful and wise, many men wanted to marry Atalanta. But Atalanta liked her life just as it was and did not want to be married. So she thought of a very clever plan. She announced she would marry the first man who could beat her in a foot race. And although her speed was famous throughout the country, many men came to race against her. But all failed to outrun the swift Atalanta.

Finally, a young man named Melanion challenged her. He was not as swift as many of the others, but he was smarter. From the end of the world, he had gotten three apples of pure gold, which no one could resist.

As the race started, Atalanta sprinted into the lead. Then Melanion rolled one of the golden apples ahead of her. Atalanta could not help stopping to pick it up, and by the time she had retrieved the apple, Melanion had caught up to her. The two runners were side by side for a moment. Then Atalanta took the lead again, and Melanion dropped the second apple. Again, Atalanta stopped to pick it up. Melanion used the last of his strength to take the lead. But when Atalanta saw Melanion ahead of her, she sprinted like the wind into the lead. Then Melanion dropped the last of the golden apples, and as Atalanta stooped to pick it up, she saw Melanion cross the finish line just ahead of her. True to her word, Atalanta married the clever Melanion, for she admired his spirit and wisdom.

Think About It
Do you think Atalanta and Melanion were happy together? Why or why not?

Atalanta is pronounced at á lan'tá.

Melanion is pronounced me lā'ni ăn.

Name _____

Atalanta and the Golden Apples

Main Idea

1. Choose another title for this story.

_____ The Race

_____ How Melanion Outsmarted Atalanta

_____ The Fastest Runner

Sequencing

2. Number the events below in the order that they happened.

_____ Kindly hunters adopted Atalanta.

_____ Melanion won by dropping the golden apples.

_____ Atalanta's father left her on a mountainside.

_____ Melanion challenged Atalanta to a race.

_____ Atalanta married Melanion.

_____ Atalanta announced she would marry the first man who could beat her in a foot race.

Reading for Details

3. Scan the story to answer these questions.

Who nursed Atalanta and raised her? _____

What plan did Atalanta think of to avoid marriage? _____

_____

Where did Melanion get the three golden apples? _____

When did Atalanta sprint like the wind? _____

Why did Atalanta marry Melanion? _____

Reading for Understanding

4. Check the correct answer(s).

I became a fast runner because

_____ I didn't weigh much.

_____ I was strong.

_____ I was raised in the wild.

I avoided marriage because

_____ I was happy with my life.

_____ I didn't like men.

_____ I was waiting for a bear.

I married Melanion because

_____ I said I would.

_____ I liked him.

_____ I admired his cleverness.

Thor Recovers his Stolen Hammer

The favorite possession of Thor, the thunder god of the Norse people, was his magic hammer, Miolnir. When he swung the great hammer, Thor caused lightning, thunder, and storms on Earth. But one morning his hammer was nowhere to be found. Thor was furious until the mischievous god, Loki, reported that he had seen a terrible storm in the land of the Giants. Thor knew that only his hammer could have made such a storm, so he ordered Loki to go to Giantland and find out who the thief was.

In the form of a bird, Loki flew until he came to a mountain top where the Giant, Thrym, sat swinging the magic hammer. Loki thought he would get the hammer by flattery, so he said, "You are so mighty that you have no need for silly hammers. Give Thor back his toy so he will leave me alone." But Thrym said he would not return the hammer until the gods sent the beautiful goddess, Freya, to be his wife.

When Thor heard Thrym's demand, he was sick with anger. How could he send Freya to be the wife of an ugly, evil Giant? But Loki had a plan. He suggested that Thor borrow Freya's clothes and dress himself as the bride, then go to Thrym's castle and try to find the hammer. Thor wasn't happy with the plan, but he agreed. The other gods and goddesses howled with laughter when they saw huge Thor dressed in dainty white robes with a veil over his head to hide his great, flowing beard.

When Thor and Loki reached the Giants' castle, Thrym was delighted to see such a fine big bride. He led the two "women" inside and set out a huge banquet for his guests. Then he announced, "Bring in Thor's hammer, for it is my wedding gift to the bride." When the servants arrived, dragging the hammer, Thor jumped up and tore off his veil. "You have stolen that from me!" he roared as he swung the hammer and brought down the walls of the castle. Then, happy that he had found his hammer, Thor went peacefully back home, vowing to never let the hammer out of his sight again!

Think About It
Why do you think Thor agreed to dress up as a bride? Would you do that if you were in his place? Why or why not?

Thor is pronounced thor.

Loki is pronounced lō'ki.

Thrym is pronounced thrim.

Freya is pronounced frȳ'a.

Miolner is pronounced my ōl'nėr.

Name _____

Thor Recovers his Stolen Hammer

Main Idea
1. Choose another title for this story.

_____ A Trip to Giantland

_____ The Mysterious Bride

_____ Thor's Magic Hammer

Sequencing
2. Number the events below in the order that they happened.

_____ Loki had a plan to get Thor's hammer back.

_____ Thor swung the hammer and brought down the walls of the castle.

_____ Thor and Loki arrived at Thrym's castle.

_____ Thor dressed up as a bride for Thrym.

_____ Thrym had Thor's hammer brought in.

_____ Thor went home peacefully.

Reading for Details
3. Scan the story to answer these questions.

Who ordered Loki to go to Giantland? _____

What caused the terrible storm in Giantland? _____

Where was Thrym swinging the hammer?_____

When was Thor sick with anger? _____

_____

Why did Thor wear a veil? _____

Reading for Understanding
4. Choose the correct word in each sentence below.

When I found out that the Giants had my hammer, I was (furious, calm).

When I heard that Thrym wanted to trade my hammer for Freya, I was (angry, amused).

When I was dressed up as a bride, I was (excited, unhappy).

When I roared at Thrym and brought down the castle walls with my hammer, I was (sad, triumphant).

When I went back home with my hammer, I was (peaceful, agitated).

Bloodstoppers

Throughout history people have told stories about men and women who have mysterious healing powers. Some of the most interesting of these tales are about the bloodstoppers.

A bloodstopper's special power is the ability to stop bleeding with the touch of a hand or by saying special words or prayers. Often, a bloodstopper can help a victim even though the bloodstopper is far away and has never seen the injured person. Many old people living in the north woods of Minnesota and Michigan have their favorite bloodstopper stories. Usually they sound much like this one told about Tom, a young Michigan farmer.

Tom and his cousin were cutting hay when the cousin slashed his arm with a scythe. It was a bad cut, right down to the bone. By the time Tom helped his cousin walk the mile to the house, his cousin was weak, and his shirt was soaked with blood. Tom tried to bandage the wound, but the bleeding wouldn't stop, and his cousin was getting weaker. Finally, Tom decided to hitch up the horses and drive seven miles to get a doctor, but he feared that by the time he got back his cousin would be dead.

On the road, he met Ben, an old man who lived in a nearby cabin. Ben saw Tom driving fast and stopped him to ask what was wrong. When he heard about the accident, Ben said, "Go back to your farm, Tom. Your cousin isn't bleeding any more."

Tom thought Ben was crazy, for he had just seen his cousin's arm pouring blood. But at Ben's insistence he went back to the farmhouse to look at his cousin. Imagine Tom's surprise to find that Ben had been right! His cousin was weak and pale, but he wasn't bleeding at all. Old Ben had been a powerful bloodstopper.

How do people get bloodstopping power? It is said to be passed from a man to a woman or from a woman to a man. Bloodstopping is also said to come naturally to people born as seventh sons of seventh sons, or seventh daughters of seventh daughters. No one knows whether bloodstopping powers are real. But some people say they wouldn't be alive today if they hadn't been cured by a bloodstopper.

Think About It
Would you want to be a bloodstopper? Why or why not?

Name _____

Bloodstoppers

Main Idea

1. This story explains

_____ how Tom's cousin cut his arm.

_____ Tom's long ride in the wagon.

_____ a bloodstopper's special power.

Sequencing

2. Number the events below in the order that they happened.

_____ Tom started out to get a doctor.

_____ Tom went back to the farmhouse to find his cousin's arm had stopped bleeding.

_____ Tom and his cousin were cutting hay.

_____ Tom's cousin cut his arm with a scythe.

_____ Tom met Ben, a bloodstopper.

_____ Tom and his cousin walked back home.

Reading for Details

3. Scan the story to answer these questions.

What special power does a bloodstopper have? _____

_____

Where was Tom going when he met Ben? _____

Why did Ben tell Tom to go back home? _____

Why do some people believe in bloodstoppers? _____

_____

Who can be a bloodstopper? _____

_____

Reading for Understanding

4. Circle yes or no.

People say I have mysterious healing powers.	Yes	No
People say I can make a person bleed by touching him/her or by saying special words or prayers.	Yes	No
People say I am a bloodstopper because I am the seventh son of my father who is the seventh son.	Yes	No
People say they believe in me because I can cure them.	Yes	No

The Rarest Bird

It is not often that people get to see the last members of an endangered species. But bird scientists, called ornithologists, on Walt Disney's Discovery Island in Florida are getting that sad opportunity. The U.S. government has given them permission to capture the last known dusky seaside sparrows in order to try and save them.

The dusky seaside sparrow used to be plentiful in the St. John River area of Florida where it lived in tidal marshes. But as people started moving into the area, the little brown bird's problems began. First, it was poison. In order to kill mosquitoes, DDT was sprayed on the marshes. No one stopped to think what the poison would do to the birds. Between 1946 and 1962, when the spraying stopped, the number of dusky seaside sparrows went down 75 per cent.

The DDT didn't kill all of the mosquitoes, so engineers from the National Aeronautics and Space Administration flooded the area to make it impossible for mosquitoes to lay eggs. The flooding did get rid of the mosquitoes, but it also destroyed nesting grounds for the birds. By 1968, only seventy known pairs of the sparrows were left. Then luck seemed to smile, for nine hundred more pairs of sparrows were found in an area which had not been explored before. But people began moving into that area too, and by 1969 the region had eight times as many people and many fewer birds than just a few years before. To make matters worse, an expressway was built through the marshes which destroyed even more of the dusky seaside sparrows' home.

Now the little "duskies," as they are called, are believed to be down to only four, and all four are males. Maybe a female or two will be found. If no females are found, ornithologists hope to crossbreed the males with female sparrows that look similar. Then, although there wouldn't really be any more duskies, in a way they would still live on.

It is much easier for people to destroy a species by carelessness than to save it with science. There were only four known dusky seaside sparrows early in 1984. There may be even fewer when you read this. There may be none.

Think About It
If you were a scientist, what would you do to save the dusky seaside sparrows?

Name _____

The Rarest Bird

Main Idea
1. Choose another title for this story.

_____ Building an Expressway

_____ Spraying DDT

_____ Destroying the "Duskies"

Sequencing
2. Number the events below in the order that they happened.

_____ DDT spray decreased the sparrow population by 75 per cent.

_____ Only four male duskies were left.

_____ The sparrows' nesting grounds were destroyed by flooding.

_____ People moving into that area destroyed the sparrows' home, destroying even more of the duskies.

_____ Nine hundred more pairs of sparrows were found in an unexplored area.

Reading for Details
3. Scan the story to answer these questions.

Where do the dusky seaside sparrows live? _____

_____

When did their problems begin? _____

_____

Why was DDT sprayed in the area?_____

_____

Who is trying to help the duskies today? _____

_____

What are they trying to do? _____

_____

Reading for Understanding
4. Place the correct letter in the blank.

_____ DDT   a. scientists who study birds

_____ ornithologists   b. sparrows living in tidal marshes

_____ "duskies"   c. a poison used to kill mosquitoes

_____ crossbreed   d. to produce an offspring from a male and female of different breeds

Euglena, the Mystery Creature

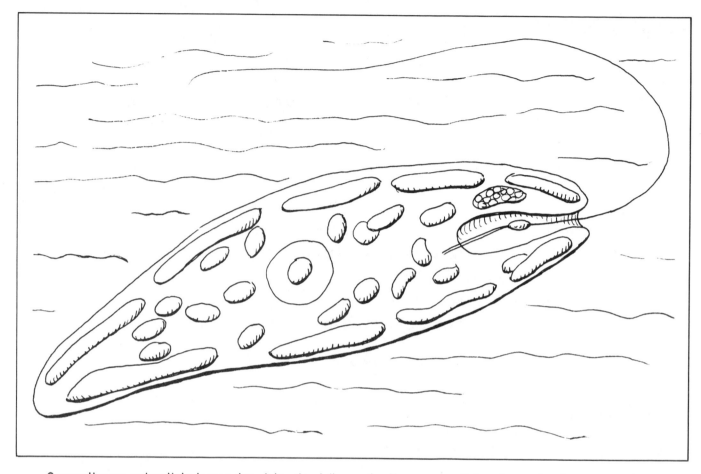

Sometimes scientists have trouble deciding whether something is a plant or an animal. Whenever they see a Euglena, they are puzzled all over again.

Usually, telling a plant from an animal isn't difficult at all. Long ago, scientists separated plants and animals into two separate kingdoms. Members of the animal kingdom move from place to place by themselves, and they must eat plants or other animals to survive. On the other hand, members of the plant kingdom cannot move very much on their own. But they make their own food. Chlorophyll, the little particles that give plants their green color, lets the plant use water and carbon dioxide gas to make sugar for food.

Euglena began causing problems for scientists long ago. It is a tiny creature that lives in pond water and swamps and can only be seen with a microscope. Its whole body is made up of one cell, and it is shaped a little like a cigar. Inside the tiny cell are grains of chlorophyll just like the chlorophyll in green plants. But Euglena also has a mouth and a gullet, a kind of stomach, and it can eat smaller plants and animals. Like many one-celled animals, Euglena swims through the water by quickly moving a long tail, called a flagellum, from side to side. Around its mouth, cilia, which look like many tiny hairs, wave back and forth to draw food into the gullet. Strangest of all, this creature has an "eye," a red spot near the flagellum that scientists say can tell light from dark.

Is Euglena a plant or an animal? Biologists, scientists who study living things, are not sure. Some think that it began as an animal that somehow absorbed some chlorophyll. Others think that it was always a plant. Most one-celled creatures are either algae, which are plants, or protozoa, which are animals. But Euglena has decided to be both. Perhaps one day someone will discover just what Euglena is. Until then, this strange creature will be a scientific mystery.

Think About It
What do you think a Euglena is–plant or animal? Why?

Name _____

Euglena, the Mystery Creature

Main Idea
1. This story tells about

_____ chlorophyll in plants.

_____ an organism that seems to be both a plant and an animal.

_____ the plant kingdom and the animal kingdom.

Sequencing
2. Number the events below in the order that they happened.

_____ Scientists found that the Euglena had characteristics of both the plant and animal kingdom.

_____ They separated plants and animals into two kingdoms.

_____ Scientists began studying the world of living things.

_____ The Euglena remains a mysterious creature to scientists.

Reading for Details
3. Scan the story to answer these questions.

What kind of scientists study the Euglena? _____

Why are they puzzled by this creature?_____

_____

What plant-like characteristics does the Euglena have? _____

_____

What animal-like characteristics does the Euglena have? _____

_____

Where does the Euglena live? _____

Reading for Understanding
4. Place the correct letter in the blank.

_____ animal kingdom   a. scientists who study living things

_____ plant kingdom   b. members cannot move very much on their own

_____ flagellum   c. gives plants their green color

_____ chlorophyll   d. one-celled animals

_____ biologists   e. a long tail

_____ algae   f. members move from place to place by themselves

_____ protozoa   g. one-celled plants

The Simplest Machines

When people think of machines, they often think of engines or motors with many moving parts. But some of the most useful machines of all have no moving parts at all. Scissors, brooms, bottle openers, and even parts of the body are all useful machines called levers.

A lever is made up of four parts that work together. First is the force that moves the second part, the weight. The weight and the force are connected by the third part, a bar called the arm. And the first three parts rest on a support called a fulcrum. Most levers have these four parts, but the parts can be placed in different ways to do different kinds of work. The different kinds of levers make up most of the simple tools we use today.

Some levers have the fulcrum between the force and the weight. A seesaw is a good example of this kind of lever. The person on the ground is the force, while the person in the air is the weight. The seesaw itself is the arm and the pipe it rests on is the fulcrum. The person on the ground pushes off and forces the person in the air down to the ground. Now that person becomes the force and the other person, who is now in the air, becomes the weight.

A wheelbarrow loaded with dirt is an example of another kind of lever. Here the weight is between the force and the fulcrum. The wheel is the fulcrum, the load of dirt is the weight, and the person pushing the wheelbarrow is the force. When the person lifts the end of the wheelbarrow and pushes, the person is using a lever to move the dirt.

Some levers help move things through great distances. In this kind of lever, the force is between the weight and the fulcrum. When you pick up a rock in your hand and bend your elbow to lift it, your arm becomes a lever. The muscles in your forearm are the force, the elbow is the fulcrum, and the rock is the weight.

Levers are older and simpler than any other machines, but they are as useful today as they were thousands of years ago when the Egyptians used them to help build the pyramids.

Think About It
What levers have you used lately?

Name _____

The Simplest Machines

Main Idea

1. Choose another title for this story.

_____ The Seesaw

_____ When Your Arm Becomes a Lever

_____ An Old and Useful Tool

Sequencing

2. Number the events below in the order necessary to explain how a lever works.

_____ The weight and the force are connected by the arm.

_____ A lever is made up of four parts that work together.

_____ The force moves the weight.

_____ The parts are the force, the weight, the arm, and the fulcrum.

_____ The force, the weight, and the arm rest on the fulcrum.

Reading for Details

3. Scan the story to answer these questions.

Why are levers useful today? _____

_____

What is a good example of a lever with the fulcrum between the force and the weight?

_____

Where is the person on the seesaw when he is the weight? _____

When does he become the force? _____

_____

How can levers be made to do different kinds of work? _____

_____

Reading for Understanding

4. Place these tools in the correct column.

knife, rake, scissors, lathe, wheelbarrow, screwdriver,
nutcracker, crowbar, drill, egg beater, wagon,
broom, bottle opener, saw, hammer, windmill,

Levers	Non-levers
_____	_____
_____	_____
_____	_____
_____	_____
_____	_____
_____	_____
_____	_____

The Unusual Behavior of Floating Ice

Think for a minute about what would happen if ice sank instead of floating on top of water. Ponds and streams would freeze solid, and fish would be trapped in the ice. Frogs, snails, and shellfish would die too, because the ice would take away the air they need to breathe. Water plants would be destroyed. And every spring when the lakes and rivers finally did thaw, they would be filled with dead plants and animals. Luckily, ice does float, but that behavior is unusual. Most liquids get heavier as they freeze, so they sink. For example, cubes of frozen alcohol would sink to the bottom of a glass of alcohol instead of floating as ice cubes do in water.

What makes ice able to float? To answer this question, you must understand what happens when things get colder. As a liquid cools, the molecules in the liquid get closer together. Because they are closer together, more molecules can fit into a space, and the liquid gets heavier. So a cold liquid is heavier than a warm liquid.

When a liquid gets cold enough, it freezes. Usually when things freeze, they become even heavier than their liquid form. But water is different. As it gets cooler, water at first acts the same as other liquids, getting heavier and heavier. When the temperature is 34° Farenheit, or 1° Celsius, water is heaviest. But then something happens. Instead of getting smaller and heavier as it freezes, water suddenly expands, or takes up more space than liquid water. You may have seen this for yourself if a bottle full of water has been left outside in the cold weather. The frozen water may have expanded so much that it sticks up out of the top of the bottle. When frozen water expands, it gets lighter. So ice can float on top of water instead of sinking to the bottom.

Most of the time it is a good thing that ice expands. But sometimes water may get into cracks in streets and roads. If the water freezes, the pressure caused by the expanding ice can break the pavement. Then the holes and cracks are expensive to repair. And if we put a full bottle of soda into the freezer to get cold quick and then forget about it, we may find the expanding ice has shattered the bottle and ruined our treat.

Think About It
Think of some other reasons floating ice is useful. When can it be harmful?

The Unusual Behavior of Floating Ice

Main Idea

1. This story explains

_____ why ice is able to float.

_____ what happens when things get colder.

_____ why you shouldn't put a bottle of soda pop in the freezer.

Sequencing

2. Number the events below in the order that they happen.

_____ The liquid gets heavier.

_____ When the liquid gets cold enough, it freezes.

_____ The molecules get closer together.

_____ The liquid cools.

_____ More molecules fit into the same space.

Reading for Details

3. Scan the story to answer these questions.

How is water different than other liquids? _____

_____

Why is ice able to float? _____

_____

When is expanding ice helpful? _____

_____

When is it harmful? _____

What would happen if ice sank in lakes and rivers? _____

_____

Reading for Understanding

4. Circle yes or no.

Water is heavier in its frozen form than in its liquid form.	Yes	No
As it cools, water gets heavier and heavier.	Yes	No
Water is heaviest at 34° Farenheit or 1° Celsius.	Yes	No
As it freezes, water suddenly explodes and floats away.	Yes	No

34°

The Story of Color

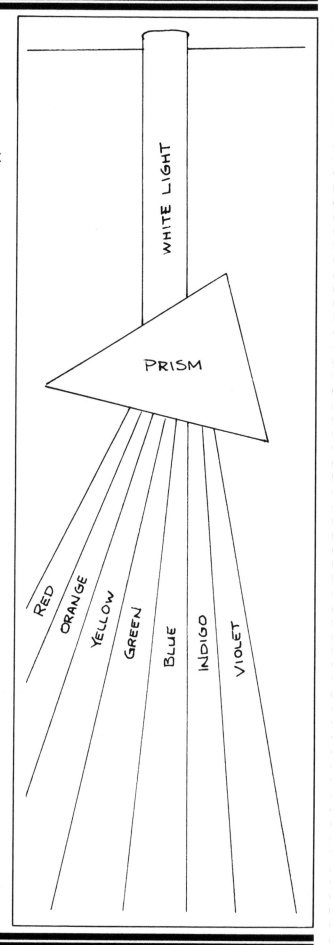

Imagine a world where everything is either black, white, or gray. Without the blue of the sky or the red of an apple, life would be dull. But if you look outside just after sunset, the colors of the buildings, trees, and sky fade. Everything does look gray. And at night, of course, the world seems to have no color at all. But you know the grass is still green at night, even though you can't see the color. Why are things colored at all and why do colors seem to change when the light changes?

Light is made up of waves, a little like waves on an ocean. Each color is a different kind of wave, and the light we see is made up of seven colors—red, orange, yellow, green, blue, indigo, and violet. Light usually looks white because all the different waves travel in different directions and mix together. But a special piece of glass, called a prism, can separate the white light into its seven colors. Raindrops sometimes act like prisms too. So when the sun shines during a rain shower, the raindrops separate the sunlight into its colors, making a rainbow.

When white light shines on an object, the object soaks up, or absorbs, some of the light. The rest of the light is bounced back, or reflected. But not all objects reflect the light in the same way. A red apple, for example, absorbs all the light waves except the red ones. It reflects the red light waves back to our eyes, so we see the color of the apple as red. An orange only reflects orange light and absorbs the rest. Grass reflects only green light waves. So the color of an object is the color of the light waves it reflects. White objects don't absorb any light at all. They reflect all of the light that strikes them. But black objects absorb all of the light that strikes them. They don't reflect any light, and no light at all makes black.

When only a little light shines on an object, it cannot reflect enough light for our eyes to see its color. That is why everything looks gray or black at night. We need the sun's light to help us see all the wonderful colors around us.

Think About It
What are three of your favorite colors? Why?

Name _____

The Story of Color

Main Idea
1. Choose another title for this story.

_____ The Colors of the Rainbow

_____ Raindrops and Other Prisms

_____ Light and Color

Sequencing
2. Number the events below in the order that they happen.

_____ The rest of the light is reflected.

_____ White light shines on an object.

_____ The object absorbs some of the light.

_____ Your eyes see the reflected light.

Reading for Details
3. Scan the story to answer these questions.

What seven colors is light made of? _____

_____

Why does light usually look white? _____

_____

When do we see color? _____

Where does the colored light reflect? _____

Why don't we see color at night? _____

Reading for Understanding
4. Place the correct letter in the blank.

_____ light   a. color of the light wave it reflects

_____ colors   b. special piece of glass which separates light into seven colors

_____ prism   c. made up of seven kinds of waves

_____ absorb   d. different kinds of light waves

_____ reflect   e. soak up

_____ color of object   f. sunlight separated into colors by raindrops

_____ rainbow   g. bounce back

A, B, and O: The Blood Group Alphabet

Sometimes people lose too much blood from injuries or accidents. To save their lives, doctors must replace the lost blood. In an operation called a transfusion, doctors put blood given by healthy people into the veins of the sick or injured person. But they must be careful. Although all blood looks the same, there are really different types of blood. Someone getting the wrong type of blood in a transfusion may become very sick or even die.

All blood is made up of red and white cells, and a liquid called plasma. It is the red cells that cause blood to be different types. On the outside of the red cells of some people's blood are proteins. Doctors group these proteins into two different classes, "A" and "B." People with the "A" protein have Type A blood, while people with the "B" protein have Type B blood. If someone happens to have both proteins, that person has Type AB blood. Some people don't have either protein, and their blood is called Type O.

If a person receives a transfusion of the wrong type of blood, the body senses the strange protein on the new blood cells. So the body destroys the new blood, and the patient goes into shock. For instance, people with Type A blood will become very sick if they are given Type B blood because their bodies try to destroy the strange Type B protein. People with Type O blood have no proteins on their cells, so their bodies will destroy both Type A and Type B blood. They can only receive Type O blood. But people with Type AB blood have both proteins, so they can receive Type A, Type B, and Type AB blood. These people are called "Universal Receivers." People of any blood type can receive Type O blood because it has no protein for the body to fight against. So Type O people are called "Universal Donors."

Doctors are always careful to test blood for its type before it is used in a transfusion. And, although the wrong type of blood can be harmful, the right type can save a life.

Think About It
Do you know your blood type? How can you find out?

Name _____

A, B, and O: The Blood Group Alphabet

Main Idea
1. Choose another title for this story.

_____ Blood Types

_____ Universal Receivers and Donors

_____ Proteins of the Blood

Sequencing
2. Number the events below in the order that they should happen.

_____ Doctors give the person a transfusion of the blood.

_____ A person loses blood from an injury or accident.

_____ The person is saved.

_____ Doctors check the person's blood type.

_____ Doctors obtain blood with the same blood type as the patient's.

Reading for Details
3. Scan the story to answer these questions.

What causes people to have different blood types? _____

_____

Where are the proteins located? _____

When does the body destroy new blood? _____

_____

Why are doctors careful when they do transfusions? _____

_____

Who are Universal Donors? _____

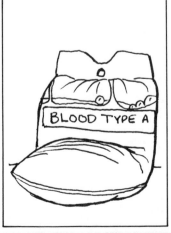

Reading for Understanding
4. Circle yes or no.

All blood has three parts; red cells, white cells, and a liquid called plastic.	Yes	No
Doctors group blood proteins into two different classes.	Yes	No
If a person has no blood proteins, her blood type is NO.	Yes	No
People with Type AB blood are called "Universal Receivers" because they can receive Type A, Type B, or Type AB blood.	Yes	No

Earthquakes—Nature at Work

Hardly anyone knows about the greatest earthquake the United States ever had. In 1811, near New Madrid, Missouri, the ground shook so hard that people 400 miles away felt the shock. Fortunately, not many people lived in the area then, so the earthquake did not cause much damage. But people in other places have not always been so lucky. An earthquake in San Francisco in 1906 killed 700 people and started a great fire that destroyed much of the city. In 1920, a quake in China killed 200,000 people in 300 square miles.

Although an earthquake can happen anywhere, there are some places that get earthquakes more often. The countries around the Pacific Ocean, for example, have many earthquakes. So do mountainous places like Italy, Turkey, and Afghanistan. Earthquakes happen because the top, or crust, of the earth is not one piece. Instead, it is made of several pieces, called plates, that move slowly. When the edges of two plates bump together or slide past each other, the vibrations can cause an earthquake. Plates come together where oceans meet the land or where mountains form, so places in these areas are most likely to have earthquakes. There are also weak spots at other places in the earth's crust. When pressure builds up under the earth, the weak spots can form cracks, or faults. The land on one side of the fault rises and the land on the other side sinks, thus causing an earthquake.

No one can predict for sure when and where an earthquake will happen. But once one starts, scientists called seismologists can tell exactly where it began. Earthquakes send vibrations for a long distance through the rocks in the earth. Sensitive instruments can measure the strength of the vibrations. Then each earthquake is given a number on the Richter Scale, which tells how much energy the earthquake had. An earthquake with a Richter number of 1.0 is too small for people to feel. A 4.5 earthquake causes windows to break and plaster to fall, while an earthquake with a Richter number of 8.0 can crumble buildings and cause great damage.

Think About It
What places in the United States are most likely to experience earthquakes?

Name _____

Earthquakes— Nature at Work

Main Idea
1. Choose another title for this story.

_____ The San Francisco Earthquake

_____ The Story of Earthquakes

_____ Measuring Earthquakes

Sequencing
2. Number the events below in the order that they happen.

_____ An earthquake occurs.

_____ Pressure builds up under the earth.

_____ Weak spots form cracks or faults.

_____ One side of the fault rises; the other side sinks.

_____ Vibrations are sent long distances through the rocks in the earth.

Reading for Details
3. Scan the story to answer these questions.

Where did the greatest U.S. earthquake take place?_____

_____

When did it happen? _____

What places in the world experience earthquakes more often? _____

_____

How do plates in the earth's crust cause an earthquake?_____

_____

Why do faults in the earth cause earthquakes? _____

_____

Why do scientists measure earthquakes?_____

_____

Reading for Understanding
4. Place the correct letter in the blank.

_____ Seismologists   a. the top of the earth

_____ Richter Scale   b. scientists who study earthquakes

_____ crust   c. cracks in the earth's surface

_____ plates   d. numbers used to tell how much energy an earthquake had

_____ faults   e. several pieces that make up the earth's crust

Accidents, Dreams, and Discoveries

Many people think that scientists make great discoveries only while they are working hard in a laboratory. But sometimes scientists, mathematicians, and inventors find the answers to difficult problems while they are relaxing or even sleeping.

For example, the great physicist Isaac Newton had been trying for a long time to discover the laws of gravity. For a while his work went well, and he worked out two of the laws. But then he seemed to come to a dead end. Finally, he decided to forget his work and relax for just one day. As he sat under an apple tree, enjoying the warm, pleasant afternoon, an apple fell from the tree and landed on the ground in front of him. Of course, Newton had seen apples fall from trees before. This time, though, the falling apple gave him the clue he needed, and the last of the laws of gravity fell into place too.

As you can see, the most ordinary things can help scientists make discoveries. Sometimes even things we usually think of as pests can be useful. The French mathematician, Rene Descartes, sat one day watching a fly walk on his ceiling. Instead of swatting the fly, he watched it cross the ceiling, come to a corner, and walk down the wall. In his imagination, Descartes drew a line following the fly's path. As the line crossed the corner of the wall, Descartes thought of the perfect way to make pictures of mathematical equations on graph paper. The method that he and the fly invented is still used today.

Sometimes even dreams can lead to inventions. Elias Howe had been trying for a long time to invent a sewing machine. But he could not quite make his machine work. After another long day of failure, Howe gave up and went to sleep. That night he dreamed that he was being chased by men carrying spears. But these strange spears had holes in their points. When Elias woke up, he remembered the dream, and his problem was solved. He put the eye of the sewing machine needle at the pointed end, and his invention worked!

Think About It
Why do you think we are sometimes able to solve difficult problems while we are relaxing?

Accidents, Dreams, and Discoveries

Main Idea

1. This story explains

   _____ how Isaac Newton discovered the third law of gravity.

   _____ how flies walk on ceilings.

   _____ how important discoveries are sometimes made during relaxation.

Sequencing

2. Number the events below in the order that they happened.

   _____ Isaac Newton developed the third law of gravity.

   _____ Isaac Newton sat under an apple tree.

   _____ Newton took the day off from work to relax.

   _____ An apple fell to the ground.

   _____ The apple gave him the clue that he needed.

Reading for Details

3. Scan the story to answer these questions.

   Who invented the sewing machine? _____

   Why had Howe given up and gone to sleep? _____

   _____

   What helped Howe solve his problem? _____

   _____

   Where were the holes in the spears that Howe dreamed about? _____

   _____

   When did Howe's invention finally work? _____

   _____

Reading for Understanding

4. Circle yes or no.

I invented a perfect way to make pictures of mathematical equations on graph paper.	Yes	No
A fly helped me.	Yes	No
I swatted the fly.	Yes	No
My method is outdated today.	Yes	No

The Pest That Can Save Lives

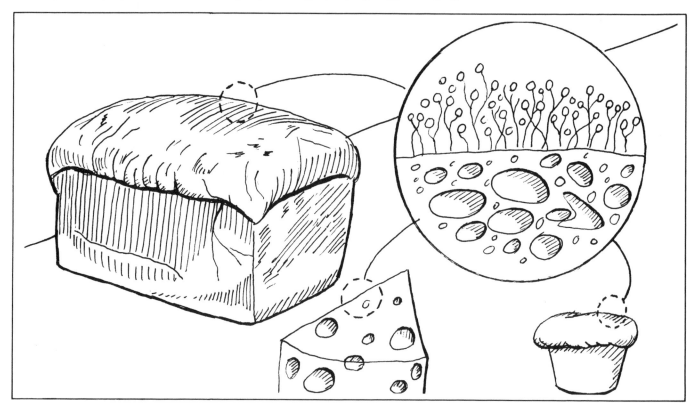

Have you ever taken a piece of bread to make toast or a sandwich and found it covered with white, fuzzy mold? Or maybe you've seen a greenish powder growing on an orange. That's mold too. Once food becomes moldy, it is ruined and must be thrown away. Mold seems to be able to grow on almost anything people eat, but where does this pest come from?

Mold is a plant in the fungus family. Fungus plants must get their food from other plants or animals. The seeds of the mold, called spores, are always in the air, but they are much too small to be seen without a microscope. When they land on some food–for example, a piece of bread–they begin to grow, much like seeds grow in soil. First hyphae, which are tiny stems, grow all along the food. Then the hyphae send down roots, called rhizoids, which burrow down into the bread. The rhizoids produce chemicals that dissolve the bread, so the mold can use it as food. With this food, the mold sends out more hyphae and rhizoids until it covers the whole piece of bread. When it begins to run out of food, the mold starts to produce its own spores. Stalks grow up from the hyphae, and on the end of each stalk is a sac that becomes filled with thousands of spores. When you see black, brown, or green mold, you are really seeing the colored sacs, because the hyphae are always white. When the sacs are full, they burst, sending the powdery spores flying into the air. Then the mold plant dies, but when the spores land on food, they become new mold plants.

It's difficult to keep mold from growing, but keeping food dry helps slow down mold's growth. Mold also doesn't grow well on foods that contain a great deal of sugar or salt. So honey, jelly, and pickles seldom get moldy.

Mold is such a nuisance that it seems strange that some mold may be helpful. But medicine made from penicillin, a relative of the green mold that grows on oranges, is used to fight disease. Medicines are made from other kinds of mold too. So although mold may spoil your favorite snack, remember that one day its cousin may help your body fight disease.

Think About It
Find out some other medicines that are made from molds. What are the medicines used for?

Name _____

The Pest That Can Save Lives

BREAD MOLD — Hyphae, SACS, RHIZOIDS

Main Idea

1. This story tells

_____ how mold grows.

_____ why honey and jelly stay fresh.

_____ how penicillin is made.

Sequencing

2. Number the events below in the order that they happen.

_____ Seeds of the mold land on food and begin to grow.

_____ The mold plant dies.

_____ Chemicals dissolve the food so that the mold plant can eat the food and grow.

_____ The mold plant produces its own spores in tiny sacs which eventually burst open.

_____ The mold plant has used all of the food and now covers the entire piece of food.

Reading for Details

3. Scan the story to answer these questions.

What kind of plant is mold? _____

Where does the mold on plants come from? _____

When does it begin to grow on food? _____

_____

When does mold begin to produce spores?_____

_____

Why is some mold helpful? _____

Penicillin MOLD

Reading for Understanding

4. Place the correct letter in the blank.

_____ mold   a. tiny stems

_____ penicillin   b. a plant in the fungus family

_____ hyphae   c. a kind of mold used to fight disease

_____ rhizoids   d. roots of the mold plant

_____ spores   e. a colored part on the end of each stalk filled with spores

_____ sacs   f. seeds of the mold plant

The Duckbilled Platypus: Nature's Experiment

In the pools and rivers of eastern Australia lives a little animal that looks like someone put it together from spare parts. Its body is furry, like a beaver's, and it has a large flat tail. But, like a duck, it has a bill and webbed feet. It swims as well as a fish and lays eggs like a bird. But unless you go to Australia, you will probably never see it, for it dies in captivity. This rare little animal is called a duckbilled platypus.

Although the platypus is a mammal, it is not very much like other mammals such as dogs or rabbits. It is a member of the family of the very first mammals, called monotremes. These animals seem to be Nature's experiment at making a mammal out of a bird or a reptile. For instance, although the platypus babies are hatched from eggs as birds are, they get their food from the mother's milk like mammal babies. A reptile's body temperature is the same as the temperature of its surroundings, and so is a monotreme's. But the monotreme has fur like a mammal.

The platypus gets along perfectly in its watery home. Its duck bill helps it dig in the mud for worms and shellfish, its favorite food. The webbed feet make the platypus an excellent swimmer under water. But like all mammals, the platypus has lungs and breathes air. How does it manage to swim under water for a long time? The answer is its special nose. Since its nostrils are near the top of its bill, the platypus keeps the end of its bill out of the water when it swims. It can breathe perfectly and still stay under water.

During the day, this timid animal digs a burrow in the mud along the riverbank. But when darkness hides it from its enemies, the platypus swims about looking for food. When the time comes for a female to lay her eggs, she builds a special burrow lined with grass and leaves. Then she lays her eggs and curls up around them to keep them warm. After her eggs hatch, the mother platypus teaches her babies to swim, find food, and avoid their enemies. Away from humans and other animals, these strange creatures live their busy, contented lives.

Think About It
Why do you think a platypus dies in captivity?

Name _____

The Duckbilled Platypus: Nature's Experiment

Main Idea

1. This story tells about

_____ a rare and unusual animal.

_____ the family of the very first mammals.

_____ a special nose.

Sequencing

2. Number the events below in the order that they happen.

_____ The female platypus lays her eggs.

_____ The female platypus builds a burrow lined with grass and leaves.

_____ The mother teaches her babies to swim.

_____ The platypus curls up around the eggs to keep them warm.

_____ The eggs hatch.

Reading for Details

3. Scan the story and answer these questions.

Where does the platypus live? _____

Why is a platypus only seen in Australia? _____

What does the body of the platypus look like? _____

When does a platypus go swimming? _____

Why does the platypus keep the end of its bill out of the water as it swims? _____

_____

Reading for Understanding

4. I am called "Nature's Experiment" because I am a mammal with characteristics of birds and reptiles. List my characteristics in the correct column.

body like a beaver, swims, has a bill, has webbed feet,
breathes with lungs, furry, lays eggs, feeds
young with own milk, body temperature same as surrounding temperature

Mammal	Reptile	Bird
_____	_____	_____
_____	_____	_____
_____	_____	_____
_____	_____	_____
_____	_____	_____

The Whooping Crane, A Bird in Danger

Many birds migrate each year, traveling south in the winter and returning north in the summer to lay their eggs and raise their families. Beyond enjoying an occasional glimpse of the birds overhead, few people pay much attention to the migrating birds. But it is a different case with whooping cranes. When these beautiful birds travel between their summer home in Canada and their winter home in Texas, biologists and bird-watchers from many countries pay very close attention to their travels.

Whooping cranes are large, white birds with black wing tips and red faces. They stand about four feet tall, with long necks and legs. Their height helps them to see great distances across the marshes where they live. To help them in their long flights, whooping cranes' wings can measure seven feet across when fully spread. But its striking appearance is not the reason this bird is so interesting to biologists. The whooping crane is in danger of becoming extinct.

Whooping cranes are shy birds who try to avoid people. But they could not escape the many hunters who gathered to shoot the birds in the 1800's and early 1900's. So many cranes were killed, that by 1940, fewer than two dozen were left! Then, concerned conservationists stepped in and persuaded the U.S. Congress to make the whooping crane an endangered species. Now it is a crime to kill these beautiful birds.

Only two baby cranes are born each year to whooping crane parents, and one of the babies often dies. So biologists have taken some of the eggs and put them in the nests of sandhill cranes. The sandhill cranes become foster parents to the whooping crane chicks. As a result, more whooping cranes will survive to start flocks of their own.

In the last few years, the number of whooping cranes has slowly increased, but this beautiful bird is still in danger of disappearing forever. However, with legal protection and the help of conservationists and biologists, it is now possible that one day the whooping crane may no longer be an endangered species.

Think About It
Why will it take a long time before the whooping crane is out of danger?

Name _____

The Whooping Crane,
A Bird in Danger

Main Idea

1. This story tells about

_____ the yearly migration of the whooping crane.

_____ the plight of the whooping crane.

_____ foster parents for the whooping crane.

Sequencing

2. Number the events below in the order that they happened.

_____ Conservationists became concerned about the whooping crane.

_____ Hunters shot many whooping cranes.

_____ The U.S. Congress declared the whooping crane an endangered species.

_____ Fewer than two dozen whooping cranes were left.

_____ It became a crime to kill whooping cranes.

Reading for Details

3. Scan the story to answer these questions.

Why is it a crime to kill the whooping crane? _____

_____

What danger threatens the whooping crane? _____

Who   trying to help the whooping crane? _____

Where do biologists put some of the whooping crane's eggs? _____

_____

Why do they do this? _____

Reading for Understanding

4. Circle yes or no.

The whooping crane is a large, pink bird.	Yes	No
It has red wing tips and a black face.	Yes	No
It stands four feet tall, has a long neck, and long legs.	Yes	No
The whooping crane's neck helps it see great distances.	Yes	No
Its wings measure seven feet across when they're spread out.	Yes	No

The Doppler Effect

Have you ever listened to a train whistle and noticed that as the train got closer, the sound of the whistle seemed to get higher? And then when the train passed you and got farther away, the pitch of its whistle seemed to get lower again. But did the sound really change? Or did you just hear the sound differently? Christian Doppler, an Austrian scientist in the early 1800's, was curious about this change in the pitch of the sound too. And because he was the first person to explain it, this phenomenon is now known as the Doppler Effect.

Doppler explained how sound is made and how it travels through the air. When something makes a sound, the air around it is vibrated. Vibrations travel through the air in waves called sound waves, much like ripples travel on a lake. All sound waves travel through the air at the same speed, and when the waves reach your ear, you hear the sound. If the waves are close together, you hear a high-pitched sound, and if the waves are far apart, the sound is low-pitched. So, for example, sound waves made by a violin are close together, while those made by a tuba are far apart.

When both you and the object making the sound are standing still, the pitch of the sound is always the same. But suppose you are standing by a railroad track. A train is coming toward you, blowing its whistle. When the train is far away, the sound waves must travel a great distance to reach your ears. As the train comes closer, though, the sound waves don't need to travel so far to reach your ears. They begin to catch up to the sound waves the whistle made when it was farther away. So the sound waves that reach your ears now are closer together than the ones you heard before, and you hear a higher-pitched sound. The closer the train gets, the higher the whistle seems to sound. After the train passes you and gets farther away, the sound waves must travel a great distance to reach your ears. And as the waves get farther and farther apart, you hear the pitch of the whistle get lower and lower until it disappears.

Think About It
What are three other sounds that demonstrate the Doppler effect?

Name _____

The Doppler Effect

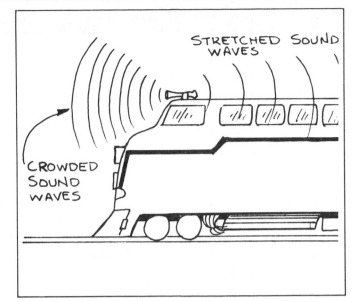

STRETCHED SOUND WAVES

CROWDED SOUND WAVES

Main Idea

1. This story explains

_____ how sound travels.

_____ why we hear different pitches from the same sound.

_____ how a train whistle sounds.

Sequencing

2. Number the events below in the order that they happen.

_____ Vibrations travel through the air in sound waves.

_____ When something makes a sound, the air around it vibrates.

_____ When the waves reach your ears, you hear sound.

Reading for Details

3. Scan the story to answer these questions.

Who was Christian Doppler?_____

Where did he live? When?_____

What did he explain? _____

_____

Why was it called the Doppler Effect? _____

_____

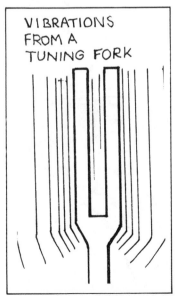

VIBRATIONS FROM A TUNING FORK

Reading for Understanding

4. Circle yes or no.

Sound waves travel through the air at different speeds.	Yes	No
Vibrations travel through the air in alpha waves.	Yes	No
Sound waves from a flute are closer together than those from a tuba.	Yes	No
As a train gets closer to you, its whistle sounds lower.	Yes	No

The Great Fire Mystery

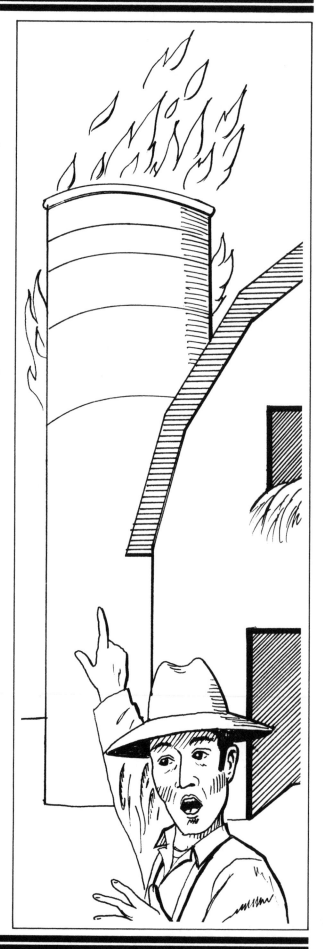

Some oily rags are packed tightly into a box and stored away in an attic. For a long time nothing happens. Then one day the box bursts into flames even though no one has come near it. A silo filled with damp grain suddenly burns down in the middle of the night when no one is around. These fires appear to be very mysterious, for they have no apparent causes. But there is one cause of fire that many people don't understand or even think about – spontaneous combustion.

All fires are caused by the heat that is given off when oxygen combines with some material – wood, paper, or cloth, for instance. This combining happens all the time to almost everything and is called oxidation. Fast oxidation gives off much heat and light very quickly and causes things to burn. Slow oxidation gives off no light and very little heat, not nearly enough to cause a fire. But when this little bit of heat is trapped, as in a tightly closed box of rags, it can not escape into the air. Instead it builds up inside the box. As more and more oxidation occurs, more heat is trapped. As the material gets hotter, it oxidizes faster, and the faster oxidation produces even more heat. Finally the rags get so hot that they can catch fire all by themselves.

Damp or oily materials are the most likely things to produce spontaneous combustion because a little moisture makes them oxidize more quickly. Powders, like sawdust, flour, or coal dust, are also dangerous. Oxygen can combine easily with these tiny particles and produce heat very quickly, causing flash fires or serious explosions.

To prevent spontaneous combustion, rags or papers to be stored should always be perfectly dry and should be packed loosely in open boxes or containers. Fires caused by spontaneous combustion have destroyed millions of dollars worth of property and have cost many lives. But knowing about spontaneous combustion and its causes can help prevent these tragedies in the future.

Think About It
Make a checklist for your home that can be used to help prevent a fire caused by spontaneous combustion.

Name _____

The Great Fire Mystery

Main Idea

1. This story explains

_____ how to store materials safely.

_____ flash fires and explosions.

_____ spontaneous combustion.

Sequencing

2. Number the events below in the order that they happen.

_____ Oily rags are packed tightly into a box.

_____ Faster oxidation produces even more heat.

_____ Spontaneous combustion occurs.

_____ Heat builds up inside the box.

Reading for Details

3. Scan the story to answer these questions.

What materials are most likely to produce spontaneous combustion? Why? _____

_____

What causes fire? _____

_____

What is oxidation? _____

Why are powders dangerous?_____

_____

How can spontaneous combustion be prevented? _____

_____

Reading for Understanding

4. Place the correct letter in the blank.

_____ oxygen combining with some material   a. slow oxidation

_____ gives off no light and very little heat   b. oxidation

_____ gives off much heat and light   c. spontaneous combustion

_____ when materials get so hot they explode into flames   d. fast oxidation

The Rain that Kills

When the rain falls, it runs into rivers and lakes or soaks into the ground, and at last flows into the oceans. From the oceans the water evaporates and rises into the air, where it forms clouds and falls to the earth as rain again. This water cycle continues day after day, year after year. Water is so important for life on earth that it is hard to imagine rain that kills the fish in the lakes and destroys plants instead of making them grow. But acid rain is causing just these problems in many parts of the world.

Acid rain is caused by gases such as sulfur dioxide and hydrogen sulfide. These gases are given off as waste by automobiles and by some factories and power plants, especially those that burn coal. These gases rise high into the air and combine with the tiny water droplets that form the clouds. When the gases and the water droplets combine, strong acids, such as sulfuric acid, form. The acids mix with other water droplets and fall to the earth as rain or snow. Acid rain doesn't look different from other rain, but it can corrode metal, eat away at buildings made of limestone or marble, and seriously damage the environment.

How does acid rain affect plants and animals? Plants use rain to make food and to grow. But acid rain can cause plants to grow much slower than if they were getting normal water. Some plants become so unhealthy after absorbing acid rain that they eventually shrivel and die. Some forests around the world have recently begun to show signs of severe damage, and many scientists suspect acid rain is the cause.

When acid rainwater flows into a lake, the water becomes more and more acidic. Most fish and water plants cannot live in very acidic water, and they die, leaving no life at all. As long as the acid remains in the lake, it cannot support life.

Scientists are still learning about acid rain, and they have not yet found a way to fix the damage it causes. But concerned people in many countries are now working to stop the causes of acid rain.

Think About It
What are at least five ways that you and your family use water every day?

Name _____

The Rain that Kills

Main Idea

1. This story tells about

_____ the water cycle.

_____ acid rain and the problems it causes.

_____ scientists learning about acid rain.

Sequencing

2. Number the events below in the order that they happen.

_____ Gases and water droplets combine to form strong acids.

_____ The acid rain corrodes metal and damages buildings.

_____ Factories and automobiles give off gases.

_____ Acids mix with water droplets and become acid rain or snow.

Reading for Details

3. Scan the story to answer these questions.

Why do plants need rain? _____

When can rain be harmful to plants? _____

What areas are beginning to show severe damage? _____

_____

Who thinks that this damage is caused by acid rain?_____

Why haven't we been able to stop the damage? _____

_____

Reading for Understanding

4. Place the correct letter in the blank.

_____ sulfur dioxide   a. form clouds

_____ environment   b. cannot live in very acidic water

_____ water droplets   c. gas given off by cars and factories

_____ fish   d. surroundings

_____ acid rain   e. dangerous gases and rain drops mixed
                              together

Shifting Continents

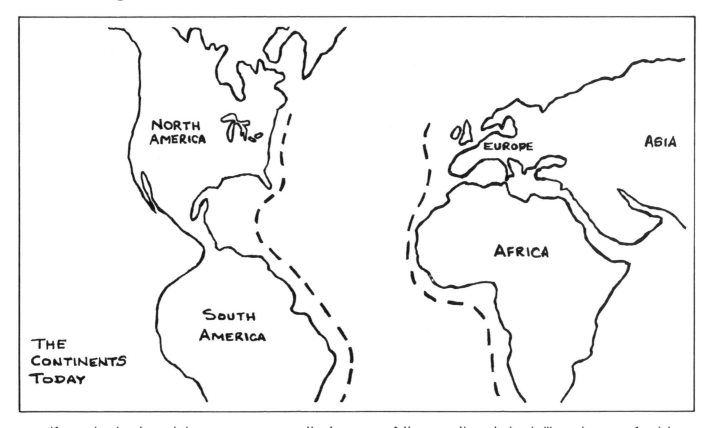

THE CONTINENTS TODAY

NORTH AMERICA

SOUTH AMERICA

EUROPE

ASIA

AFRICA

If you look at a globe, you can see that some of the continents look like pieces of a big jigsaw puzzle. Geologists, or earth scientists, think that millions of years ago all the continents were connected to make one big super-continent.

For a long time, no one was able to explain how the continents had split apart, if they had once really been connected. Then a man named Alfred Wegener developed a theory called Continental Drift to explain why there are now seven continents instead of one. He said the inside of the earth is composed of magma, a thick liquid made up of melted rock. The top, or crust, of the earth is made up of large plates that float on top of the magma. At one time, the plates carrying the continents were joined together into a huge land mass, called Pangaea. The rest of the world was one great ocean. But some of the magma rose up through the ocean and formed some new crust. This caused pressure on the big land mass and broke it into two pieces. One piece was made up of the continents of what are now Europe, Asia, and North America. The other piece included present-day Africa, South America, Australia, and Antartica. As more magma rose up, the two large pieces of land gradually broke up again into the continents we know today. The movement of the magma inside the earth carried the continents away from each other, much as a current in a river pushes a boat along.

What kind of evidence do geologists have that the continents were once connected? Certain rock structures in Africa and South America are so much alike that they must once have been part of the same formation. Also, scientists have found fossils of the same plants and animals on continents that are now far apart. But the best proof of the continental drift theory is that it is still happening today. Scientists say that fifty million years from now, the Atlantic Ocean will be much wider than it is now. Africa and Europe will touch each other, the Mediterranean Sea will almost disappear, and North and South America will not be connected to each other at all!

Think About It
Why is the Continental Drift theory important?

Name _____

Shifting Continents

Main Idea

1. Choose another title for this story.

_____ The Earth's Crust

_____ The Earth–A Big Jigsaw Puzzle

_____ The Continental Drift Theory

Sequencing

2. Number the events below in the order that they happened.

_____ The two large pieces gradually broke up into the continents of today.

_____ Movement of magma carried the continents away from each other.

_____ The continents were joined into a huge land mass.

_____ Pangaea broke into two pieces.

_____ Magma rose up through the ocean and formed new crust.

Reading for Details

3. Scan the story to answer these questions.

Who developed the Continental Drift theory? _____

What evidence is there that the continents were once connected? _____

_____

When do geologists think that all the continents were connected? _____

_____

What continents made up one of the two pieces of broken Pangaea? _____

_____

When do geologists predict that the Atlantic Ocean will be wider than it is today? _____

_____

Reading for Understanding

4. Place the correct letter in the blank.

_____ Pangaea

_____ Continental Drift

_____ fossils

_____ crust

_____ magma

_____ geologists

a. theory that explains why there are seven continents instead of one

b. ancient remains of plants and animals

c. name of huge land mass formed by all the continents

d. thick liquid of melted rock

e. scientists who study the earth

f. top layer of the earth

The Hungry Brain

Many people think that an empty stomach causes hunger. This idea seems to make sense, for when we are hungry, our stomachs rumble and hurt. We head to the refrigerator for a snack, and in a little while our stomachs stop hurting and feel full. But it's a small area called the hypothalamus, deep inside the brain, that really tells us to be hungry.

Scientists found out about the hypothalamus and hunger by doing experiments with rats. They carefully put a very thin wire inside the rat's brain and into the hypothalamus. The rat didn't seem to be uncomfortable. In fact, it didn't seem to notice that the wire was there at all. Then the scientists sent a very weak electric current through the wire. When the rat received the current in a certain part of the hypothalamus, it would eat and keep on eating even though its stomach was full. If scientists moved the wire to a different part of the hypothalamus and again sent a current down the wire, the rat would not eat at all. It acted as though it was not hungry, even if it hadn't eaten anything in several days. This showed the scientists that different parts of the hypothalamus control the feelings of being hungry or full.

In real life, of course, people and animals don't have wires sending electric currents through their brains. So how does the hypothalamus really work to cause or stop hunger? The blood tells the hypothalamus what to do. Many blood vessels flow into the hypothalamus. When the blood is not carrying many nutrients for the cells in the body, the hypothalamus senses that the body will soon run out of energy. It then sends signals that cause the stomach to secrete digestive juices and to start churning. The animal or person feels hungry and goes to look for food. When the blood contains enough nutrients, the hypothalamus stops sending signals to the stomach, which then stops churning. The quiet stomach causes a feeling of being full. So, strange as it may seem, hunger comes from the brain.

Think About It
What are your favorite snacks when you are hungry?

Name _____

The Hungry Brain

HYPOTHALAMUS

Main Idea
1. This story explains

_____ how the brain controls hunger feelings.

_____ that rats are used for scientific experiments.

_____ why blood runs through the brain.

Sequencing
2. Number the events below in the order that they happen.

_____ Blood vessels in the hypothalamus don't have enough nutrients.

_____ The animal or person feels hungry.

_____ The hypothalamus sends signals to the stomach to start churning.

_____ The hypothalamus senses that the body will soon run out of energy.

_____ The hypothalamus stops sending signals when the blood has enough nutrients.

Reading for Details
3. Scan the story to answer these questions.

What part of the brain controls hunger? _____

What did scientists use to study hunger feelings? _____

_____

Where did scientists put the thin wire? _____

When would the rat eat even though its stomach was full? _____

_____

Why would the hungry rat refuse to eat? _____

_____

Reading for Understanding
4. Choose the topic for each paragraph.

Paragraph 2

_____ Experiments with rats helped scientists learn about hunger feelings.

_____ Electric currents are used in experiments with rats.

_____ Rats are not hurt in scientific experiments.

Paragraph 3

_____ People don't have wires in their brains.

_____ A quiet stomach is a full stomach.

_____ Several parts of the body are involved in sensing hunger.

The Mighty Virus

Often you will hear someone who has a cold or the flu say, "It's just a virus." But the virus deserves more respect because it is one of the most strange and troublesome creatures in the world.

Viruses are too small to be seen with an ordinary microscope, and they can pass through filters that trap very tiny particles. So for many years no one even knew that viruses existed. Even after they were discovered, scientists didn't know for a long time whether or not viruses were alive. A virus is made up of only a core of DNA or RNA, chemicals which help it to reproduce, and a coating of protein. When the virus is outside of a living animal or plant, it seems like just a chemical crystal. It doesn't eat, breathe, or grow.

But when a virus meets a living cell, it begins to come alive. Its protein coat now acts like a little plunger and pushes the virus' DNA into a cell. Once it is inside the host cell, the DNA of the virus combines with the cell's DNA and takes control. The virus forces the cell to produce more viruses identical to the invading virus. When the cell becomes full of viruses, it bursts, and each virus finds a new cell in the body to invade. The plant or animal the virus has attacked becomes sick.

Many plants, such as tobacco and tomatoes, can be destroyed by viral diseases. And viruses cause disease in almost every kind of animal, including worms, chickens, dogs, and humans. Fortunately, some viral diseases can be prevented. Doctors have found a way to weaken or kill some viruses. When healthy people receive small doses of a virus in the form of vaccinations, they will not get the disease caused by that virus.

If a person does get a viral disease, there is really no cure except rest, since medicines do not usually work against viruses. Luckily, most viruses die quickly and the patient soon gets well.

Think About It
Beside vaccinations, what are some things that you can do to prevent a viral infection?

Name _____

The Mighty Virus

Main Idea
1. This story tells about

_____ viruses.

_____ chemical crystals.

_____ DNA and RNA.

Sequencing
2. Number the events below in the order that they happen.

_____ The plant or animal the virus has attacked becomes sick.

_____ A virus meets a living cell.

_____ The cell produces more viruses just like the invading virus.

_____ The virus' DNA combines with the cell's DNA.

_____ The protein coat pushes the virus' DNA into a cell.

Reading for Details
3. Scan the story to answer these questions.

What is a virus made of? _____

_____

What does DNA and RNA do for a virus? _____

_____

When does a virus come alive? _____

What are two ways to fight viruses? _____

Why is it lucky that most viruses die quickly? _____

_____

Reading for Understanding
4. Place the correct letter in the blank.

_____ protein coat   a. state of a virus outside of a living plant or animal

_____ tomatoes   b. weak virus given to people to prevent diseases

_____ vaccination   c. pushes the virus' DNA into a living cell

_____ chemical crystal   d. can be destroyed by viral disease

pH—The Chemist's Tool

You may have seen television commercials that advertise "pH balanced shampoos," or heard that water had a neutral pH. But what exactly does pH mean? What kinds of things have a pH?

Scientists can divide almost all liquids into two groups–acids and bases. Acids taste sour and contain many hydrogen atoms. Some acids, like hydrochloric acid and sulfuric acid, are very dangerous and must be handled carefully. Others, like orange juice and vinegar, are harmless and can even help to keep our bodies healthy. Bases, on the other hand, have a bitter taste and contain a combination of hydrogen and oxygen atoms called hydroxyl groups. Strong bases like lye, which is mixed with fat to make soap, can cause serious burns. But weak bases, taken from the leaves and stems of plants, are sometimes used in manufacturing medicines.

Chemists use many different kinds of acids and bases in their work. Because it is important for them to know how strong each acid or base is, they invented a measurement called pH. The pH of a liquid tells whether it is an acid or a base, and just how weak or strong it is. A liquid can have a pH number from 1, the strongest acid, to 14, the strongest base. Any solution with a pH less than 7 is an acid, while a solution with a pH greater than 7 is a base. But what about solutions with a pH of 7? They contain equal numbers of hydrogen atoms and hydroxyl groups, so they are neither acids nor bases. They are said to be chemically neutral. Pure water is one of the few substances whose pH is 7.

Even though our bodies contain a great deal of water, we do not have a pH of exactly 7. Chemicals produced in the body are slightly acidic or basic, so different parts of the body may have slightly different pH's. Blood, for example, has a pH of just a little more than 7, while the pH of perspiration is slightly less than 7.

Chemists use complicated electronic instruments to measure pH, but students in chemistry classes often use litmus paper to get a rough idea of a liquid's pH. Most litmus paper will turn a shade of red to indicate a liquid is an acid, and a bluish color to indicate a base.

Think About It
How could you find out whether everyday liquids such as shampoo, soap, milk, and soup are acids or bases. Why might you want to know?

Name _____

pH—The Chemist's Tool

LITMUS PAPER

Main Idea
1. This story explains

_____ what hydroxyl groups are.

_____ what pH means.

_____ what chemists do with acids and bases.

Sequencing
2. Number the events below in the order that you read about them.

_____ Chemists invented a measurement called pH.

_____ Chemists need to know how strong each acid or base is.

_____ Scientists divide liquids into two groups–acids and bases.

_____ Chemists use many different acids and bases in their work.

_____ We use pH to tell whether a liquid is an acid or base.

Reading for Details
3. Scan the story to answer these questions.

What are two characteristics of acids? _____

_____

What are two characteristics of bases? _____

_____

What is the pH level of acids? of bases?_____

_____

What liquids are chemically neutral? _____

What does acid do to litmus paper? How about bases? _____

_____

VINEGAR   FROZEN ORANGE JUICE

Reading for Understanding
4. Write "acid" or "base" in each blank.

vinegar _____   perspiration _____

lye _____   blood _____

orange juice _____   leaves and stems _____

Your Body's Fright Reaction

You have probably noticed that when you're watching a scary movie, when you are startled by a loud noise, or when you think about doing something unpleasant, your heart begins to beat very fast. You know your heartbeat speeds up when you are very active, but this time you haven't been running or exercising at all. So what causes such a fast heartbeat?

It all begins with your brain. All parts of the body are connected to the brain by nerves. Some nerves carry signals from the body to the brain, while others carry orders from the brain out to the organs, such as the heart and lungs, and to the muscles. When you see, hear, or even think of something that frightens you or makes you nervous, your brain begins sending signals to special glands in your body, called the adrenal glands, which are located on top of each of the two kidneys. Like other glands, the adrenals produce small amounts of chemicals which the body needs at certain times. As soon as they receive signals from the brain, the adrenals secrete a chemical called epinephrine directly into the bloodstream. When the epinephrine reaches the heart, it causes the heart to beat faster and harder. This makes the blood carry more oxygen and food to the cells, giving the body extra energy, either to run away from or to fight whatever frightens you. When the danger passes, the brain stops sending signals to the adrenals, and they stop producing epinephrine. Your heart slows down to normal again.

Epinephrine causes other changes to take place in the body too. It makes you breathe faster and sends more blood to the muscles and less to the skin and stomach. That is why you will often feel cold when you're nervous or frightened. Epinephrine also causes your hands to perspire, so you could get a better grip on a weapon if you need one. All of these changes make your body ready for action. So even if you never take a step to run away or raise a hand to fight, your brain helps your body to be ready – just in case.

Think About It
Write about an experience that frightened you. Describe your fright reaction.

Name _____

Your Body's Fright Reaction

Main Idea
1. Choose another title for this story.

_____ When Your Heart Beats Fast

_____ The Adrenal Glands

_____ How Your Body Prepares for Danger

Sequencing
2. Number the events below in the order that they happened.

_____ The heart beats faster and harder.

_____ When there is danger, the brain sends signals to the adrenals.

_____ The blood carries more oxygen and food to the cells.

_____ The adrenals secrete epinephrine into the bloodstream.

_____ When the danger passes, the brain stops sending signals to the adrenals.

_____ The body receives extra energy to respond to the danger.

Reading for Details
3. Scan the story to answer these questions.

What happens to your heartbeat when you are frightened? _____

_____

Why does your heart need to beat faster? _____

_____

What makes your heart beat faster? _____

_____

What other changes take place in your body when you are frightened?_____

_____

Which organ controls your body's fright reaction? _____

Reading for Understanding
4. Place the correct letter in the blank.

_____ adrenal   a. a chemical secreted by the adrenals

_____ signal   b. fluid emitted by a gland

_____ epinephrine   c. a gland on top of the kidney

_____ nerves   d. a message

_____ secretion   e. carry signals between the body and the brain

They Came from the North

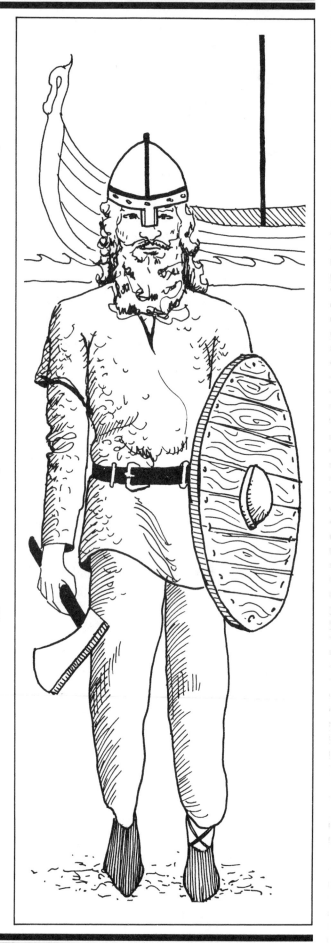

In about the year 800 A.D. a bold people lived in the countries now called Norway, Sweden, and Denmark. They were the Vikings, and as the years went by they spread their way of life to countries all over the world.

Their native countries were cold and barren, but they were close to the sea. So the Vikings became great sailors and ventured far from home in search of riches. Many were pirates, plundering other lands, but some were traders as well. In their long ships, the Vikings sailed far away from their northern home. Some of them traveled westward to England, Scotland, and Ireland where they raided towns and churches for their gold. Some came to Iceland, Greenland, and what is now Newfoundland in Canada. Still others went east into Russia and as far as Turkey.

Some of the raiders did not return home. Instead, they settled in the countries they conquered. Normandy, in northern France, was settled by Vikings and, in fact, is named for the "North Men." In 874, three Viking brothers founded the kingdom of Gardarike, out of which later grew Russia. Some Vikings settled in Scotland where they adopted many of the native Celtic customs, such as wearing the kilt and tartan.

But it was the Vikings' westward journeys that are the most amazing. In their long open dragon ships they went to Iceland and started settlements there. Then they moved farther west across the cold North Atlantic to Greenland. In that harsh climate they kept settlements alive until the late 1300's. Some Vikings sailed as far west as Newfoundland. Their settlement did not last, but the ruins of those settlements still stand.

Thought of by many as pirates and warriors, Vikings were good farmers and skilled craftsmen. And for three hundred years they were the world's best sailors. Their sea voyages greatly influenced the developing cultures of many countries.

Think About It
Why do you think the settlement in Newfoundland didn't last?

Name _____

They Came from the North

Main Idea
1. This story explains

_____ how the Vikings were fierce warriors and pirates.

_____ how the Vikings influenced many cultures.

_____ why the Vikings were not satisfied with their homeland.

Sequencing
2. Number the events below in the order that they happened.

_____ The Vikings began to move further west on their journeys.

_____ They raided towns and churches in search of gold.

_____ Vikings sailed away from their homes in search of riches.

_____ Many countries still show the influence of the Viking culture.

_____ Some of the Vikings began to settle in the countries they conquered.

Reading for Details
3. Scan the story to answer these questions.

What countries were conquered by the Vikings? _____

_____

What were the Vikings looking for? _____

When did three Viking brothers found Gardarike? _____

Who adopted the Celtic custom of wearing the kilt and the tartan? _____

_____

Why were the Vikings able to travel so easily? _____

_____

Reading for Understanding
4. Circle yes or no.

The country I was born in was cold and bountiful.	Yes	No
I was a trader.	Yes	No
I traveled west to England, Scotland, and Iran.	Yes	No
Others that I knew went east into Russia and Turkey.	Yes	No

Canada's National Sport

Most people think that Canada's national sport is ice hockey. Although hockey is played everywhere in Canada and Canadian players are among the best in the world, lacrosse is Canada's official national sport. In 1867, shortly after the birth of Canada, the Canadian Parliament made lacrosse the national game.

There is no game that deserves the honor more. Before Europeans came to Canada, lacrosse was played by Indians, who called it "baggataway." When the French settlers saw the game, they called it "lacrosse," because the stick used in the game looked like the hooked staff carried by bishops in the church.

The modern game of lacrosse is played by two teams of ten or twelve players each. The field is similar in size to a football field with goals at each end of the field. The players each carry a stick with a sort of basket on the end. They carry, throw, or hit a ball of hard rubber with their sticks. The object of the game is to get the ball into the other team's goal, and each goal is worth one point. Players may pass the ball with their sticks or kick the ball, but only the goal keeper may touch the ball with the hands.

Lacrosse players wear shorts, padded gloves, and arm pads, as well as helmets with face guards. Like hockey, checking is allowed, and there are penalties. Players must leave the game for one to three minutes for committing fouls.

There is another lacrosse game called box lacrosse, played on a court with boards on its sides, like ice hockey. Both the court and the goals are smaller than in field lacrosse. The rules are much the same as in the larger game, except that the ball may be played off the boards.

Both box lacrosse and field lacrosse are popular in Canada and in the eastern United States. Several universities have teams who meet every year to determine the best lacrosse team of all.

Think About It
Think of three reasons why hockey and lacrosse are popular games in Canada.

Name _____

Canada's National Sport

Main Idea

1. This story explains

_____ the history of lacrosse.

_____ the game of lacrosse.

_____ Canada's love of lacrosse.

Sequencing

2. Number the events below in the order that they happened.

_____ The Indians played a game called "baggataway."

_____ Lacrosse became the national game of Canada.

_____ The French settlers called the game "lacrosse."

Reading for Details

3. Scan the story to answer these questions.

When did lacrosse become the national sport? _____

Where are the goals on the lacrosse playing field?_____

When must a player leave the game? _____

What is another lacrosse game?_____

How is this game different from lacrosse? _____

_____

What is another sport that is played everywhere in Canada? _____

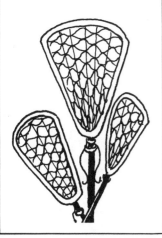

Reading for Understanding

4. Circle yes or no.

Lacrosse is played by two teams of twelve or twenty players.	Yes	No
The field is about the size of a football field.	Yes	No
The players use a stick with a box on the end.	Yes	No
The object of the game is to get the ball in your goal and make two points.	Yes	No
The players wear shorts, padded gloves, arm pads, and helmets.	Yes	No

Naming the Months

Like many of our traditions, the names of the months come to us from the ancient Romans. In 46 B.C., Emperor Julius Caesar borrowed a calendar with 365 days and 12 months from the Greeks. Fifty years later, the Emperor Augustus made the calendar official through the whole Roman Empire.

Although the Romans borrowed a Greek calendar, they used their own names for the months. This caused a problem. The Roman year began on March 1, but in the new calendar, the year began in January. The Romans never bothered to change the names to fit the change in the year, so some of the names seem strange to us today.

Starting with the beginning of the old calendar, which began the year in spring, March takes its name from the Roman god of war, Mars. No one is sure what April means or where it comes from, but people have several ideas about the words May and June. Some say May is named for the Greek goddess Maia, and that June is named for the Roman goddess Juno. Others feel that these months were named to honor the old and the young. May might come from "maiores," meaning "elders," and June from "juniores," or "youth."

July is named after Julius Caesar himself. August was called "Sextilis," the sixth month from March, until Augustus became emperor. He wanted a month named after himself, too, so he changed the name of Sextilis to August. September means the seventh month and October comes from the Roman word for eighth month. November and December are named in the same way, meaning the ninth and tenth months.

January is named for the two-faced Roman god Janus. When it became the first month, Caesar gave it 31 days to make it important. February comes from the Latin word meaning "to cleanse." In ancient Rome, February was a time of cleaning and purifying temples to prepare for the spring festivals. It once had 30 days, but both Julius and Augustus took days from it to make their months longer.

Our calendar today has changed a little from the one Julius Caesar established over 2,000 years ago, but we still use the same names for the months as the Romans did long ago.

Think About It
Do you think we should change the beginning of the year to March? Why or why not?

Naming the Months

Main Idea

1. This story explains

_____ why some months have 31 days.

_____ how the Greeks and Romans cooperated.

_____ how the months were named.

Sequencing

2. Number the events below in the order that they happened.

_____ Julius Caesar borrowed a calendar from the Greeks.

_____ Julius Caesar named July after himself.

_____ Augustus became Emperor.

_____ Augustus made the calendar official.

Reading for Details

3. Scan the story to answer these questions.

Who was emperor when the Romans borrowed the Greek calendar? _____

Where did the Romans get the names for their new calendar? _____

_____

When was the Greek calendar made official? _____

What was the main difference between the Greek and Roman calendars? _____

_____

Why did both Julius Caesar and Augustus Caesar shorten February? _____

_____

Reading for Understanding

4. Place the correct letter in the blank.

_____ March   a. named for Julius Caesar

_____ May   b. means to cleanse

_____ June   c. named for the Roman god of war, Mars

_____ July   d. means seventh month

_____ September e. named for the greek goddess, Maia

_____ October   f. means tenth month

_____ November   g. named for the Roman goddess, Juno

_____ December   h. means eighth month

_____ February   i. means ninth month

The Domesday Book

About the year 490 A.D., the Angles and the Saxons, who were people from Germany, came to England. As the years went by, their power grew until they not only ruled England, but became known as the true English people. Although they had a king, most Anglo-Saxons paid more attention to their war leaders. After all, it was these chiefs who protected them from their enemies and made laws. The people were loyal to their leaders and paid taxes to them instead of to the king. Everyone was happy with this system. But life suddenly changed for the Anglo-Saxons, for all at once a new kind of king ruled the land.

In 1066, a Frenchman called William the Conqueror invaded England with his soldiers and made himself king. He didn't trust the Anglo-Saxons, and he wanted to make sure his rule was strong. So William gave his own followers the farms that had belonged to the Anglo-Saxon leaders. Then William demanded that everyone, Anglo-Saxon and French alike, pay taxes to him. But William wanted to make sure everyone was paying enough taxes. So he ordered a list to be made of the value of all land, crops, buildings, and animals in England. This record became known as the Domesday Book.

To get this huge amount of information, William sent commissioners to every part of England. In each county, the commissioners talked to the sheriff, the priest, a landowner, and six peasants, or poor workers, to find out who owned the land. The commissioners also asked how much the land was worth and how many animals were on it. Everything was listed in the Domesday Book, acre by acre and animal by animal. Now the king knew exactly how much his kingdom was worth, and he began to tax people as heavily as he could.

Today, the Domesday Book shows how people lived in the early days of England. It is not only a tax record, but also a great history. The careful details about the people of early England and their belongings let modern people imagine the work and problems of ordinary people of those days long ago.

Think About It
Why did William want to tax the people so heavily?

Name _____

The Domesday Book

Main Idea

1. This story explains

_____ how William the Conqueror became King of England.

_____ how the Domesday Book came to be.

_____ how people lived in the early days of England.

Sequencing

2. Number the events below in the order that they happened.

_____ Information was recorded in the Domesday Book.

_____ William the Conqueror demanded that everyone pay taxes to him.

_____ William sent commissioners to each county to gather information.

_____ William the Conqueror invaded England.

_____ William the Conqueror became King of England.

Reading for Details

3. Scan the story to answer these questions.

Who came to England in 490 A.D.? _____

Where did they come from?_____

What did they give to their war leaders? _____

When did William the Conqueror invade England?_____

Why did life change for the Anglo-Saxons? _____

_____

Reading for Understanding

4. Circle yes or no.

I went to every country in Europe.	Yes	No
I talked to the sheriff, the priest, a landowner, and six peasants.	Yes	No
I asked how much the land was worth and how many houses were on it.	Yes	No
I wrote everything down in the Domesday Book.	Yes	No
I ended up with not only a tax record for the king, but a great history book.	Yes	No

The Story of Glass

What would the world be like if all the glass were to disappear? People with poor eyesight would have no glasses. There would be no microscopes, telescopes, or cameras. Bottles and jars would have to be made of metal or plastic, and windows would have no window panes. But only six hundred years ago, glass was so scarce that it was as valuable as gold. If a rich nobleman wanted to use his best plates at a dinner, he brought out his glass plates instead of his silver ones.

Glassmaking is an art that is hundreds of years old, but glass is made today in much the same way as it was centuries ago. The first glass ever made was soda-lime glass, and most of the glass made today is still this kind. Since this glass is inexpensive and easy to melt, it is used to make most windows, bottles, lamps, and table glassware.

Several materials are used in glassmaking. Silica, or ordinary sand, is most important. Chemical compounds such as soda, limestone, and lead can also go into special kinds of glass. The silica and other materials are melted together and then cooled, forming a smooth clear mass. Although glass is hard, it is not a solid, but is really a very cold, thick liquid. Some heavy glasses will change their shapes over long periods of time. This is why you may have seen old glass window panes that have "run" or sagged with age.

Lead glass is made by using lead oxide in place of lime to produce glass of fine quality. Lead glass is used to make lenses for eyeglasses, telescopes, and microscopes. Radio and television tubes as well as the tubing in neon signs are also made with this glass.

Besides being useful, glass can also be very beautiful. Glassmakers in Venice, Italy learned hundreds of years ago to swirl colors through their glass. No two pieces of this glass have exactly the same pattern of colors, and Venetian glass is still popular today for its beauty.

Glass is so much a part of our lives that it is hard to imagine life without it. It has made life easier and prettier for hundreds of years.

Think About It
What would you miss most if there were no glass today?

Name _____

The Story of Glass

Main Idea

1. This story explains

_____ life without glass.

_____ the material used in glassmaking.

_____ a short history of glass.

Sequencing

2. Number the events below in the order that they happen.

_____ The materials are cooled.

_____ Silica and other materials are melted together.

_____ They form a cold, thick liquid.

_____ Products are made from the glass.

Reading for Details

3. Scan the story to answer these questions.

When was glass as valuable as gold?_____

What kind of glass is usually made today? _____

Where did glassmakers first learn to swirl colors through their glass? _____

Why is glass an important part of our lives? _____

_____

Why does some glass change its shape over time? _____

_____

Reading for Understanding

4. Place the word or phrase in the correct column.

inexpensive, fine quality, very beautiful, made centuries ago,
used to make lenses for eyeglasses, no two pieces are the same,
used to make windows, used to make radio and TV tubes, popular today

Soda-lime Glass	Lead Glass	Venetian Glass
_____	_____	_____
_____	_____	_____
_____	_____	_____
_____	_____	_____
_____	_____	_____

The Knights of Japan

Have you ever seen swords and suits of armor in a museum? About 600 years ago, knights throughout Europe dressed in armor and hung great swords at their sides. Many people don't know that on the other side of the world, in Japan, there were knights in armor, too. These knights were called samurai, and they were very powerful men.

Not just anyone could become a samurai warrior. There were great samurai families, and only the sons of these families could be samurai. The honor of being a warrior was passed down from father to son. Each family served one nobleman. The samurai promised to protect the nobleman and to fight for him. In return, the nobleman gave the samurai land and money, and paid for his armor, sword, and horse. The samurai had other privileges too. Of all the people in Japan, only the samurai could carry weapons. If a samurai was traveling, he could ask to stay the night in anyone's home, for no one dared to keep him out.

Because they were born to be warriors, boys began their training while they were very young. Special teachers taught the boys how to ride horses and how to fight. They spent many years learning to lead armies and plan battles. But a young samurai did not just learn fighting. He had to learn to behave like a samurai gentleman. Music, poetry, writing, and art lessons were part of a samurai's training. He also learned to suffer pain silently and, most important, to be loyal. A samurai never surrendered and never did anything to make a nobleman ashamed of him.

One of the most important things a young samurai learned was how to care for his sword. A samurai was more proud of his sword than anything he owned. Each sword took months to make, for the metal had to be heated and cooled many times to make it strong. The swordmaker said special prayers at every step so that the sword would be perfect when it was finished. If he was not satisfied, the sword maker would destroy the sword and start all over again.

After many years, the noblemen lost power, and the samurai became less important. But many of their swords are in museums and collections today to remind us of the glory and courage of the samurai warriors.

Think About It
Would you want to be a samurai warrior? Why or why not?

Name _____

The Knights of Japan

Main Idea

1. Choose another title for this story.

_____ Born to be Warriors

_____ How to Care for a Samurai Sword

_____ The Samurai

Sequencing

2. Number the events below in the order that they happened.

_____ Boys were born into samurai families.

_____ The boys entered training when they were still young.

_____ Special teachers taught the boys skills needed to be a good samurai.

_____ After training, the samurai promised to protect the nobleman and to fight for him.

_____ In return, the nobleman gave many things to the samurai.

Reading for Details

3. Scan the story to answer these questions.

When did knights dress in armor?_____

What were Japanese knights called? _____

How did someone get to be a samurai? _____

_____

What things were part of a samurai's training? _____

_____

Why did the samurai's sword maker say special prayers? _____

_____

Reading for Understanding

4. Circle yes or no.

Because I am the son of a samurai warrior, I am learning how to fight.	Yes	No
I am also learning how to be a gentleman.	Yes	No
I have to learn how to endure pain loudly.	Yes	No
I must not be loyal, surrender, or shame a nobleman.	Yes	No
My most important possession is my sword.	Yes	No

Poetry—The Rhythm of Words

Everyone knows at least one poem. Little children learn nursery rhymes like "Mary Had a Little-Lamb" before they go to school. Later, they say little poems when they play games like jump rope and hide-and-seek. Poems can be simple, like the ones that start, "Roses are red, violets are blue." Or they can fill whole books and use language that is sometimes very hard to understand.

What makes poetry different from the way we speak every day? Poetry can take many forms, but its most important feature is its rhythm. No one knows who wrote the first poem, but we do know that people danced before they had a spoken language. They invented drums to beat out the rhythms of their dances. When people began to speak words, they fit the words to the rhythm of the drums, and chanting was invented. Later, when people began to play other musical instruments, the chants became songs.

At first, the songs and dances were prayers or magic spells to help keep away evil. Parents taught the songs to their children, and so they were passed from generation to generation. Much later, people began to make up songs for special occasions, like a victory in battle, or the death of a king. As time went on, these songs then grew into long stories of adventures of great heroes. They were a kind of musical mixture of history and mythology. Special performers called bards would sing them from memory.

Around 500 B.C. the Greeks wrote down the words of two long songs, The Iliad and The Odyssey. They tell about the adventures of a hero named Odysseus as he fights a great battle and then returns home. Once the words of songs were written down, they became separate from the music, and pure poetry was born. But poetry still kept its rhythm. At first most poems were about heroes or adventures. These long story-poems were called epics. But later people started writing poetry just for its beauty. They wrote about nature, or a friend, or about their deep feelings like love or sorrow.

Today, poetry may tell a story, describe a scene, or tell about emotions. Some poems rhyme, and some don't. But even now, after thousands of years, poetry would not be poetry without its rhythm.

Think About It
Write a poem of your own.

Poetry— The Rhythm of Words

Name _____

Main Idea

1. This story explains

_____ how poetry got its rhythm.

_____ how poetry is different from music.

_____ the history of poetry.

Sequencing

2. Number the events below in the order that they happened.

_____ The songs and dances were prayers or magic spells.

_____ Bards would sing these stories from memory.

_____ The songs grew into long stories.

_____ People began to make songs for special occasions.

_____ Pure poetry was born when the songs were written down and became separate from the music.

Reading for Details

3. Scan the story to answer these questions.

What is the most important feature of poetry? _____

How did poetry first get its rhythm? _____

What were most poems about at first? _____

When did the Greeks write down The Iliad and The Odyssey? _____

Why did people write poetry later? _____

_____

Reading for Understanding

4. Place the correct letter in the blank.

_____ drums   a. long story-poems

_____ chants   b. instrument for beating out rhythm of dances

_____ bards   c. words that fit the rhythm of the drums

_____ Odysseus   d. Greek hero in two long songs

_____ epics   e. special performers who would sing long stories from memory

Heroes and Messengers

Of the many mysteries in nature, the homing pigeon's ability to find its way home from hundreds of miles away is one of the most fascinating. Nobody is really sure how the pigeon navigates. Over the years, though, this ability has served humans well.

For a long time, homing pigeons were used to carry messages, particularly during wartime. The United States Army Signal Corps used pigeons until 1956. During World War II, several British Army pigeons even received medals. Before the invention of the telegraph, pigeons were used for all kinds of fast communication. And even today, there is a major corporation in California that uses homing pigeons to carry microfilm from one plant to another. The distance between the two plants is twenty-five miles by pigeon and fifty miles by car. The pigeons can cover the distance in half an hour, much faster than a car could get from one place to the other. And the total cost of this special messenger service is fifty dollars in pigeon food per year!

Perhaps the most common use for homing pigeons today is racing. People have raced pigeons since the 17th century. When pigeons were no longer as important as messengers, people began racing them more often, and pigeon racing is now popular in Britain, France, and the Netherlands. But nowhere is it more popular than in Belgium.

Before a pigeon race begins, each pigeon is taken an equal distance from its home. The bird is released, and the starting time is written down. When the pigeon gets home, the owner takes a rubber ring, called a band, from the pigeon's leg and puts it into a special clock which records the time the pigeon finished the race. The clocks are taken to the racing club where the starting and finishing times are recorded. The bird with the fastest time wins.

The homing pigeon is sometimes called the poor man's racehorse. A person can raise several pigeons for about $400 a year, and a good racer can win $15,000 to $20,000 for its owner in its life. So even though no one can figure out how a pigeon finds its way home, this special talent has benefited people for a long time.

Think About It
Pretend you are two miles from your house and have to get back by yourself. How would you do it?

Name _____

Heroes and Messengers

Main Idea

1. Choose another title for this story.

_____ By Pigeon or By Car

_____ Pigeons in World War II

_____ The Talented Pigeon

Sequencing

2. Number the events below in the order that they happen.

_____ The owner puts the band in a special clock to record the finishing time.

_____ Each pigeon is taken an equal distance from its home.

_____ The clocks are taken to the racing club, and the times are recorded.

_____ The bird is released, and the starting time is written down.

_____ When the pigeon gets home, the owner takes the band off the pigeon's leg.

Reading for Details

3. Scan the story to answer these questions.

What special ability does the pigeon have that makes it useful to humans? _____

_____

When were pigeons used for carrying messages? _____

What is the most popular use of pigeons today?_____

Where is pigeon racing especially popular?_____

Why is a pigeon called a poor man's race horse? _____

_____

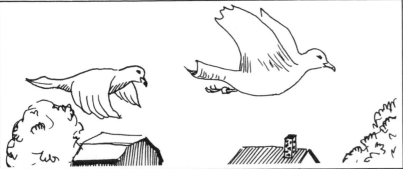

Reading for Understanding

4. What is the topic of Paragraph 4?

_____ winning races

_____ pigeon racing

_____ timing the race

The Story of the Harpsichord

When you first see one of these musical instruments, you might think it's a small piano. But a harpsichord is quite different from a piano. A piano key, when struck, hits a string with a small hammer. When you strike a harpsichord key, however, the string is plucked, much like a guitar string.

The keys of the harpsichord are connected to jacks which pluck the strings. On each jack is a quill and a damper. The quill plucks the string and the damper stops the string's sound when the key is released. Often, a harpsichord has two sets of strings. A player may play one set at a time or both sets at a time.

Harpsichords in their present shape didn't really exist before the sixteenth century. The harpsichord started as an instrument called a virginal which looked like a very small piano. Then the virginal gradually changed into a bigger instrument, the spinet. Finally, the spinet became the harpsichord that we know today. Once it grew to its full size, the harpsichord became very popular. In the sixteenth through eighteenth centuries, it was very important in European music. Nearly every musician knew how to play the harpsichord well, and it was usually the first instrument a musician learned to play. Most of the great composers of that time, like Bach, Handel, and Mozart, wrote music for the harpsichord. It was used constantly to accompany other instruments and singers in symphonies, operas, and church music.

But by the end of the eighteenth century, the piano was starting to take the place of the harpsichord. One of the harpsichord's faults was that it could not sound louder or softer. No matter how hard the player struck the keys, the sound was the same. But the piano's sound could vary. In fact, the full name of the piano is "pianoforte," from the Italian words "piano" (soft) and "forte" (loud). Gradually, the piano became king, and the wonderful harpsichord spent most of the nineteenth century in silence. But today many musicians want to play music from the past on the instruments the music was written for. So, thanks to them, the delicate sounds of the harpsichord are now being heard again.

Think About It
What kinds of instruments do you like to play or listen to? Why?

Name _____

The Story of
the Harpsichord

Main Idea
1. Choose another title for this story.

_____ The Piano Becomes King

_____ The Forerunner of the Piano

_____ European Musical Instruments

Sequencing
2. Number the events below in the order that they happened.

_____ The spinet grew to the full-sized harpsichord.

_____ The harpsichord became a very popular instrument.

_____ The virginal gradually changed to the larger spinet.

_____ The harpsichord began as an instrument called a virginal.

_____ The piano replaced the harpsichord.

Reading for Details
3. Scan the story to answer these questions.

Who were some of the great composers of the 16th-18th centuries? _____

_____

What instrument did they write music for?_____

When did people first play the harpsichord? _____

What was one of the harpsichord's faults? _____

Why did the piano become more popular than the harpsichord? _____

_____

Reading for Understanding
4. Place the correct letter in the blank.

_____ virginal   a. Italian word meaning soft

_____ spinet   b. full name of the piano

_____ pianoforte   c. developed from the virginal

_____ piano   d. Italian word meaning loud

_____ forte   e. the earliest harpsichord

The Golden People

The Aztecs were some of the most powerful and important Indian people ever to live in North America. Although no one knows exactly where the Aztecs came from, their own legends say that they traveled from somewhere in the north to settle in a valley in Mexico. They conquered the Toltecs, an Indian tribe which had been living in the valley, and grew in power until they ruled much of Mexico.

Near Mexico City, tourists can still see traces of the Aztec civilization. Their great flat-topped stone pyramids stand today as they did hundreds of years ago. These pyramids are said to have been used as altars where the Aztec priests made sacrifices to the gods. The great Aztec capital, Tenochtitlan, was built 167 years before Columbus first sailed to America, and it became the beginning of today's capital city of Mexico. Besides being expert builders, the Aztecs were skilled astronomers, rulers, and artists. The priests, who were also the astronomers, knew a great deal about the paths of the stars in the sky, and invented a complicated calendar that even today's scientists envy.

The Aztecs were also wonderfully skilled artists who worked with gold. Not only did they make earrings, necklaces, and bracelets, but they also used gold to make dishes, toys, and even shoes! The Aztec rulers wore headdresses and cloaks made of beautiful feathers and trimmed with silver, gold, and jewels.

The Aztecs were usually a peaceful people. They loved animals and flowers, and their cities were full of magnificent gardens. The people were fond of music, dancing, and literature. But they were also brave warriors who would fight to protect their civilization. When the Spanish soldier, Cortez, came to Mexico with his troops, the Aztecs and their ruler, Montezuma, welcomed them peacefully. But Cortez held Montezuma prisoner and demanded that the Aztecs give all their gold to save Montezuma's life. Although the Aztecs fought bravely, Cortez conquered them in the year 1519. The Aztec empire ended, but its rich history and skillful people are still remembered today.

Think About It
Why do you think Cortez was able to conquer the Aztecs?

96

Name _____

The Golden People

Main Idea
1. Choose another title for this story.

_____ An Empire Remembered Today

_____ The Art of the Aztecs

_____ A History of Mexico

Sequencing
2. Number the events below in the order that they happened.

_____ Cortez and his troops came to Mexico.

_____ Cortez held Montezuma prisoner.

_____ The Aztecs fought against Cortez.

_____ The Aztecs settled in a valley in Mexico.

_____ Cortez conquered the Aztecs.

Reading for Details
3. Scan the story to answer these questions.

Who lived in the Mexican valley before the Aztecs? _____

When did the Aztecs build their capital city? _____

_____

What did the Aztec artists make? _____

What materials did they like to use? _____

How did the Aztecs show they were a peaceful people?_____

_____

Why did the Aztecs fight the Spanish? _____

_____

Reading for Understanding
4. Place the correct letter in the blank.

_____ Aztecs   a. used as altars by the Aztec priests

_____ Montezuma   b. aztec ruler

_____ Tenochtitlan   c. also astronomers who invented a complicated calendar

_____ Pyramids   d. great Aztec capital city

_____ Priests   e. a powerful Indian tribe in North America

An International Game

On pleasant afternoons in countries as different as England, Australia, India, and Jamaica, children and adults grab their bats and balls, and run out to the fields to play. But these aren't baseballs or baseball bats, and it isn't a baseball field, for many people in these countries play cricket.

Cricket is similar to baseball in many ways. In both sports, the object of the game is to score more runs than the other team. In each game, one team fields while the other team bats.

But unlike baseball, in cricket the team has eleven players. Instead of having a pitcher, a cricket team has a bowler. The bowler pitches the ball to one batter, but there are actually two batters on the field at one time. Though there are only two innings in a cricket game, some games have lasted for more than two days!

Cricket started in England many centuries ago. Shepherds in the south of England used their staffs as bats. Eventually, rules were made and the game gained popularity. When the British Empire started to grow, the English people went to India, Australia, North America, and many countries in the West Indies, bringing their customs with them. When these countries became independent and the British left, many of their traditions, including cricket, stayed behind.

Cricket was once popular in the United States and Canada in the 1800's. But during the American Civil War, baseball gained popularity in the United States because it was easier to find a place to play baseball than a place to play cricket, which needs more room. So soldiers brought baseball back from the war.

Many countries have professional cricket teams. Popular cricket players are national heroes, and a few have even been knighted by the Queen of England! Cricket lovers from Jamaica to New Zealand and from India to England have made their game one of the world's most popular sports.

Think About It
Would you like to play cricket? Why or why not?

An International Game

Main Idea

1. This story tells about

_____ the game of baseball.

_____ people who play cricket.

_____ the game of cricket.

Sequencing

2. Number the events below in the order that they happened.

_____ The countries became independent.

_____ Shepherds in England used their staffs as bats.

_____ The British people brought cricket to many countries.

_____ Cricket gained popularity in England when rules were made.

_____ The countries continued to play cricket.

Reading for Details

3. Scan the story to answer these questions.

Who has made cricket one of the world's most popular sports? _____

_____

Where do cricket lovers live? _____

When was cricket popular in the U.S. and Canada? _____

What other game became popular during the Civil War? _____

Why did this happen?_____

Reading for Understanding

4. Write "B" if the item describes only baseball. Write "C" if it describes only cricket. Write "both" if the item describes both cricket and baseball.

_____ Winner is the team who scores the most runs.

_____ has a bowler

_____ nine players on a team

_____ one team fields while the other team bats

_____ has a pitcher

_____ two batters at one time

_____ nine innings

_____ one batter at a time

_____ two innings

_____ eleven players on a team

The Family of Words

Perhaps your family has a "family tree," a history of your parents, grandparents, and ancestors back as far as anyone can remember. Words have family trees too, called etymologies. Etymologists are word detectives who search through the languages of many countries, going back hundreds or thousands of years, to find out where a word comes from.

Many words in English have complicated etymologies, because English is not really one language. It started as the language of the Anglo-Saxons, people who came to England from Germany in the 5th century. France invaded England in 1066, and many French words eventually found their way into the developing English language. But French itself came from Latin, so many Latin words became part of English. The Greek language had been closely allied with Latin for centuries, and most of the scholarly and literary words in English, such as "etymology," are derived from Greek.

Later, words from even farther away began popping up in English. Under the plain Anglo-Saxon word "food" are grouped items with names from around the world. The word "coffee" comes to English from Arabia. "Chocolate" started out as the South American Indian word "cacahuatl," and "tea" is derived from the ancient Chinese words "d'a" or "cha."

Very few of the foreign words in the English language have stayed exactly as they started. As foreign words were used more often, and as the written language became more uniform, the pronunciation and spelling of these words gradually changed.

Over the years, the meanings of many words have changed too. For instance, the word "salary," which mean regular payment for doing a job, has a long history. It came to English from the French word "salarie," but the French word comes from the Latin word, "salarium," which was the money given to Roman soldiers to buy salt. ("Sal" means salt in Latin.) In the days of the Romans, salt was so scarce that it was very valuable, and Roman soldiers spent much of their money on salt. So today, when someone is paid a salary, that person is really getting money with which to buy salt!

Think About It
Find out the etymologies of these common words: mother, beef, camp.

Name _____

The Family of Words

Main Idea

1. This story tells about

_____ the study of words.

_____ the changing meaning of words.

_____ words in the English language.

Sequencing

2. Number the events below in the order that they happened.

_____ English started as the language of the Anglo-Saxons.

_____ Pronunciation and spellings changed.

_____ France invaded England.

_____ Foreign words were used more often.

_____ Many French words found their way into the English language.

Reading for Details

3. Scan the story to answer these questions.

Who are word detectives? _____

What do they do? _____

_____

Why have few of the foreign words in the English language stayed exactly the same? _____

_____

What did the word "salary" originally mean? _____

_____

What does the word "salary" mean now?_____

Reading for Understanding

4. Place the correct letter in the blank.

_____ Etymology   a. comes from Latin and French

_____ Coffee   b. comes from Greek

_____ Chocolate   c. comes from Arabia

_____ Tea   d. comes from South American Indian word "cacahuatl"

_____ Salary   e. comes from ancient Chinese words "d'a" or "cha"

Ancient Sign of Friendship

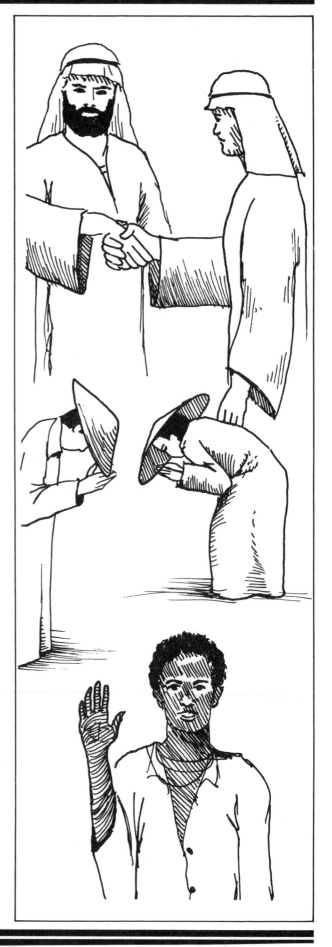

Today when we meet someone for the first time or when we greet an old friend, often the first thing we do is shake hands. The handshake has been a custom for many hundreds of years. But how did this custom start? Why is the handshake a sign of friendship?

Extending the hand in goodwill probably started thousands of years ago with primitive people. The times were dangerous and uncivilized. People carried rocks or clubs in their hands as weapons. When a traveler met another person on a road or in a forest, he couldn't be sure if the stranger would attack or be friendly. So the traveler would put out his hand toward the stranger to show that he had no weapons and did not wish to fight.

The practice of clasping or shaking hands may have many origins. Soldiers of ancient Rome shook hands by clasping each other's arms just below the elbow, and this greeting was one that no one but the soldiers could use. It was once the custom among Arabs for a lower-class person to show respect by kissing the hand of a superior person. As time went on, this practice changed to a simple clasping of hands, so that neither person would feel inferior.

The practice of clasping the right hand in friendship may have begun with the Greeks, who held out their right hands to strangers as a sign of friendship. In the Middle Ages, during the time of knights in armor, many people in Europe wore swords at their sides. When two people clasped their right hands, they were making sure that the other person could not draw his sword.

Although we take shaking hands for granted, many people in the world use different kinds of greetings. In China and Japan, bowing may take the place of the handshake, while in India a person may touch his fingertips together when meeting a person of high rank. Some African people raise one arm when they greet a friend, but they do not shake hands. And in some European countries, people may greet each other by kissing each other's cheeks; first one, and then the other. But no matter how people around the world greet each other, they are all showing signs of friendliness.

Think About It
Besides handshaking, what are some other ways that you greet your friends?

Ancient Sign of Friendship

Main Idea

1. Choose another title for this story.

_____ Customs in Many Countries

_____ Knights in Armor

_____ The Handshake and Other Signs of Friendliness

Sequencing

2. Number the sentences below in the order that you read about them.

_____ Roman soldiers clasped each other's arms in greeting.

_____ People in Japan or China may bow instead of shaking hands.

_____ Knights in the Middle Ages clasped right hands.

_____ Primitive people extended their empty hands to show they didn't wish to fight.

_____ Arabs clasped hands so neither person would feel inferior.

Reading for Details

3. Scan the story to answer these questions.

Who may have begun the practice of clasping right hands? _____

_____

Where does a person sometimes touch his fingertips together to show respect? _____

_____

Who raises one arm in greeting a friend? _____

How do some Europeans greet each other? _____

Reading for Understanding

4. Why did these people shake hands? Place the correct letter in the blank.

_____ Primitive traveler

_____ Roman soldier

_____ Arabs

_____ Knights

a. to show respect by kissing a superior person's hand

b. had a special greeting only he could use

c. to make sure that each could not draw his sword

d. to show that he had no weapons

A New Way of Life

It's a long, long journey from Canada to Louisiana, and to the Acadians, the trip seemed to carry them into another world. For over one hundred and fifty years these French people had farmed the valleys of Acadia, an area that included modern-day Nova Scotia and part of New Brunswick, in Canada. They cleared the land and drained the marshes along the Atlantic Ocean, building special dikes to keep the ocean from washing back onto the land. They raised cattle and grew flax, which they cleaned and spun to make their linen coats and the starched white caps and kerchiefs the women wore. The Acadians lived simply, much as their grandparents had lived in France, keeping the French language and old customs alive.

But in both Europe and North America, France and Britain were at war. In 1755 the British defeated the French, and Acadia came under British control. The new British governor feared a rebellion, because many of these colonists were still loyal to France. So the Acadians were forced to leave their farms, to make way for British settlers. Some went to other parts of Canada and a few managed to hide and stay in Acadia. But most Acadians were sent to find new homes in the French colony of Louisiana.

The land the Acadians found in Louisiana was very different from the rolling valleys and the cold Atlantic they had known in their old home. Here they found swamps choked with weeds and flowers, and slow, steamy rivers, called bayous. They had been farmers in Acadia. Now they learned to navigate the bayous in narrow boats called pirogues, fishing and trapping muskrats.

Over time, the pronunciation of the name, Acadians, changed to Cajuns. Today, many Cajun descendents of the travelers from Canada still live throughout southern Louisiana. The Cajuns are especially known for their style of cooking. Cajun cooking is usually hot or spicy and most often contains fish or game animals.

The French-Canadian folk customs and traditions which the Acadians brought with them on their long trip have enriched the local culture, and live on today in their Cajun descendants.

Think About It
Would you like to try some Cajun cooking? Why or why not? How could you find out more about the French-Canadian folk customs and traditions passed on through the Cajun descendants?

Cajun is pronounced kā′jun.

Name _____

A New Way of Life

Main Idea
1. Choose another title for this story.

_____ A New Governor

_____ Louisiana Settlers

_____ The Cajuns

Sequencing
2. Number the events below in the order that they happened.

_____ The Acadians were forced to leave Acadia.

_____ The British defeated the French.

_____ French people farmed the valleys of Acadia.

_____ Acadia came under British control.

_____ The Acadians moved to Louisiana.

Reading for Details
3. Scan the story to answer these questions.

What modern-day provinces made up Acadia? _____

_____

When did French Acadia come under British control? _____

_____

Why were the Acadians sent to Louisiana? _____

_____

What did the Acadians do in Louisiana instead of farming? _____

_____

Who are the Cajuns? _____

What are the Cajuns especially known for? _____

Reading for Understanding
4. Place the correct letter in the blank.

_____ bayous   a. wall built to keep out water

_____ flax   b. a narrow boat

_____ dike   c. spun to make linen

_____ pirogue   d. slow, steamy rivers

_____ Cajuns   e. new name of Acadians

The Big Sound

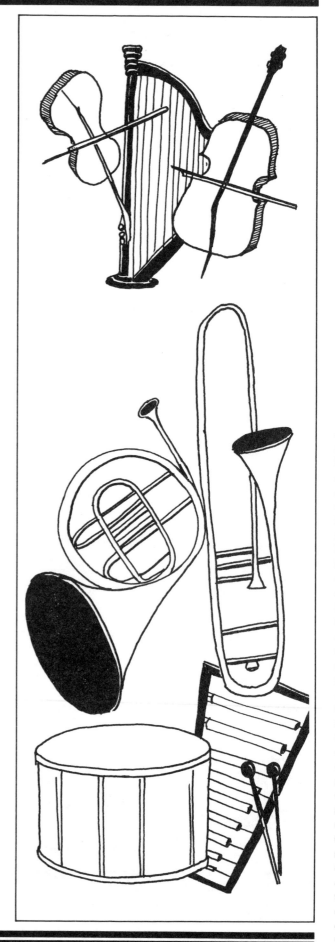

The sound of a symphony orchestra can fill a whole building and make it ring with music. But this beautiful sound that can be joyful or sad, exciting or soothing, is the result of careful planning and cooperation. Just as painters choose different colors and textures of paint for their works of art, composers choose the sounds of different instruments to produce their music. Each of the four groups of instruments – strings, woodwinds, brass, and percussion – has its special part to play in helping a symphony orchestra make the composer's music come to life.

The most important group, and the largest, is the strings. The average string section has about thirty-four violins, twelve violas, ten cellos, six double basses, and one harp. The strings set the mood of a piece of music, playing lively, bouncy tunes or sweet, sad melodies. Together the string instruments give the orchestra a base for the other instruments to build upon.

The woodwinds add color to the sound. There are four each of flutes, oboes, clarinets, and bassoons. Sometimes a flute player may also play a piccolo or an oboe player may double on the English horn. The woodwinds make the flowing, sweet sounds that make us think of wind, water, or bird songs.

The brass instruments – usually six French horns, four trumpets, four trombones, and a tuba – give the orchestra life. The trumpets add brightness and make us think of battles or royal processions, while the other brass give the orchestra a deep, full sound.

The loudest instruments in the percussion section are the four kettle drums. But many bells, drums, and chimes are also found in the percussion section. Percussion instruments add special effects. Thundering drums can make the music sound threatening, but a bell or triangle can create a delicate, airy mood.

But the purpose of a symphony orchestra is not to play section by section. After all, the word "symphony" means "sounding together." And when all the instruments play together under the direction of the conductor, their varied tones and moods create the stirring, wonderful music that only cooperation can achieve.

Think About It
Why is cooperation important in a symphony orchestra?

The Big Sound

Main Idea
1. Choose another title for this story.

_____ Sounding Together

_____ The Symphony Orchestra

_____ How Painters and Composers are Alike

Sequencing
2. Number these sentences in the order you read about them.

_____ The woodwinds add color to the sound.

_____ All instruments play together.

_____ Percussion instruments add special effects.

_____ The strings set the mood of the piece.

_____ The brass instruments give the orchestra life.

Reading for Details
3. Scan the story to answer these questions.

Who writes the music for a symphony orchestra? _____

What is the largest and most important group in a symphony? _____

_____

Which instruments make flowing, sweet sounds? _____

What is the purpose of a symphony orchestra? _____

How many instruments are usually in the symphony orchestra? (Do not include the extra

percussion instruments.)_____

Reading for Understanding
4. Place each of these instruments in the correct column.

violins, French horns, drums, flutes, violas, trumpet, bells,
oboes, cellos, trombones, chimes, clarinets, basses, bassoons, harp, tuba

Woodwinds	Strings	Brass	Percussion

The Wall the Romans Built

In northern England, near the border of Scotland, a wall runs along the hills and valleys of the countryside. Grass and weeds grow out of the cracks in the wall, and in places it has toppled over and crumbled with age. Farmers have stolen its stones to build walls of their own. Anyone looking at this ruin today would find it hard to believe that this wall was once the pride of the Romans.

The Romans first invaded Britain in the year 43 A.D. With their great armies and excellent planning, they quickly defeated the native Celtic people. Then they set about building forts, roads, and cities so that they could make their new colony as much like Rome as possible. The Celts had never seen such wide, straight roads or grand buildings, and in a few years many of them began to live like the Romans. Some of the Celts even served in the Roman army.

But the soldiers of Rome had not succeeded in conquering the whole island of Britain. Far to the north in the rugged hills lived a fierce people called Picts. The Picts had lived in Britain even before the Celts, and they were savage fighters. Not only did they refuse to be conquered, but they often came down from the north to attack the Romans. Their raids became so troublesome that the Roman emperor Hadrian finally ordered a wall to be built in the north to keep the Picts away.

Hadrian's Wall took seven years to build. It was 118 kilometers, or 74 miles, long, and about 8 feet, or 2.5 meters, thick. Sixteen large forts were placed along the wall, with many smaller forts between them. The wall was as tall as three men, and large ditches in front of and behind the wall helped keep the Picts away. For more than two hundred years Roman soldiers manned the forts, keeping the cities of the south safe from the Picts.

But then the great Roman Empire began to lose its power. In 383, the Roman soliders were called back to Rome to fight other wars, and they never returned. Today Hadrian's Wall stands in the sleepy English farmland as a reminder of the days long ago when Rome ruled Britain.

Think About It

Why do you think Hadrian's Wall was the pride of the Romans for 200 years?

The Wall
the Romans Built

Main Idea
1. Choose another title for this story.

_____ The Story of Hadrian's Wall

_____ The Invasion of Britain

_____ The Fighting Picts

Sequencing
2. Number the events below in the order that they happened.

_____ Roman soldiers manned the forts along the wall.

_____ The Romans invaded Britain.

_____ Hadrian's Wall was built.

_____ The Picts attacked the Romans.

_____ The Picts refused to be conquered.

_____ The Roman soldiers left Britain.

Reading for Details
3. Scan the story to answer these questions.

When did the Romans invade Britain? _____

Who accepted the Roman's rule quickly? _____

Where did the Picts live? _____

Why did Hadrian order a wall built? _____

Why were there ditches along the wall? _____

Reading for Understanding
4. Circle yes or no

Hadrian's wall took seventeen years to build.	Yes	No
It was 118 kilometers or 74 miles long.	Yes	No
It was 8 feet or 2.5 meters thick.	Yes	No
No one needed to take care of the wall.	Yes	No
In 383 the wall was abandoned.	Yes	No

Curds and Whey

One day, thousands of years ago, an Arab lad riding through the desert had a lucky accident that gave the world one of its most popular foods. He had put some milk in a bag made from the stomach of a sheep so that he might have something to drink on his journey. As he rode on, however, the day grew hot and the bag bounced up and down on his horse's saddle. When he opened the bag, he found not liquid milk but a solid lump of cheese.

Today's cheesemakers don't use goatskin bags to make their cheese, but they need to have all the conditions that the Arab youth had long ago. For milk or cream to turn into cheese, it needs heat, stirring, bacteria, and a chemical called rennet. Whether cheese is made at home or at a huge dairy, the milk goes through the same steps on its way to becoming cheese.

First, bacteria are added to the milk, which is heated a little to help the bacteria grow. Different bacteria give cheeses their different flavors. So, for example, cheddar cheese bacteria are different from cream cheese bacteria. When the bacteria have grown enough, rennet is added to the milk. Rennet is a digestive juice produced by sheep and cattle, and it makes the milk separate into a solid curd and a watery liquid called whey. The whey is then poured off as waste or is used as food for cattle. The curd is cut into pieces, stirred to remove more whey, salted, and put into molds to press out the very last of the whey.

When the cheese is solid and dry, it is taken out of the mold, covered with wax or wrapped in cloth to help keep out mold, and left to age. Aging helps improve the flavor of the cheese, and the longer the cheese ages, the sharper its flavor becomes. Some cheddar cheeses, for example, age up to three years before they are sold.

Today, there are hundreds of different kinds of cheeses made all over the world. Many countries have at least one favorite cheese which is made nowhere else. And while cheese is a healthful food, supplying protein and calcium, most people eat it just because they love the way it tastes.

Think About It
What are some of your favorite kinds of cheese? Where are they made?

Curds and Whey

Main Idea

1. This story tells about

_____ making cheese.

_____ the ingredients in cheese.

_____ different kinds of cheese.

Sequencing

2. Number the events below in the order that they happen.

_____ The whey is poured off.

_____ Bacteria are added to the milk.

_____ The curd is cut into pieces and pressed into a mold.

_____ Rennet is added to the milk.

_____ When the cheese is solid and dry, it is taken out of the mold.

_____ The cheese is wrapped and left to age.

Reading for Details

3. Scan the story to answer these questions.

Who had a lucky accident? _____

What did he put into his bag? _____

When did he find a lump of cheese? _____

What is added to milk to turn it into cheese? _____

_____

Why do most people eat cheese? _____

Reading for Understanding

4. Place the correct letter in the blank.

_____ bacteria   a. the watery liquid left when milk separates

_____ aging   b. give cheese different flavors

_____ whey   c. a digestive juice produced by sheep and cattle

_____ rennet   d. helps improve the flavor of cheese

_____ curd   e. solid part left when milk separates

Surveying—Mapmaking and More

When you look at a map and see the different lines and shapes of the hills, roads, and rivers, you are seeing the results of surveying–the art and science of measuring the land. When people think of surveyors working in the woods or along the roads, they often think only of map-making. But there are many other reasons for making surveys.

One valuable service surveyors perform is determining where property lines are, so that people can know who owns a piece of land. Another kind of survey, which is really two surveys in one, is done when someone wants to build a building, railway, or road. First, surveyors go out to the proposed site of the building or route of the railway or road. They make measurements of the "ups and downs" of the land and of the distances that will be covered in the project. Then they use this information to make two kinds of drawings. One is a map showing where the building or the route of the railway or road will be. The other drawing, called an elevation, shows the view from the side. This view shows how much earth has to be removed or added before construction can begin.

The surveyors then go back into the field and "lay out" the project, using precision instruments to measure the distances and angles drawn out in the design. They mark the distances and corners with wooden stakes. At that point construction can begin.

Surveys are made for other reasons too. Sometimes it becomes necessary to know how much water is in a lake or a pond, so surveyors measure its size. There are surveyors who help plan mines, and others who map the bottoms of lakes, rivers, and oceans to find the dangerous shallow places that could sink a ship or a barge.

Over the years, surveyors have charted the landscape of the country. So, the next time you use a map, think of all the careful, precise measurements surveyors have taken to help you reach your destination.

Think About It
Why do surveyors need to be precise?

112

Name _____

Surveying— Mapmaking and More

Main Idea

1. This story explains

_____ using surveys for construction.

_____ different reasons for making surveys.

_____ how maps are made.

Sequencing

2. Number the events below in the order that they happen.

_____ Surveyors go out to the proposed site.

_____ Surveyors make two kinds of drawings.

_____ Someone wants to build a road, building, or railway.

_____ Surveyors take measurements of the land.

_____ Construction can begin.

_____ Surveyors go back into the field and lay out the project.

Reading for Details

3. Scan the story to answer these questions.

When do you see the result of surveying? _____

What are some services performed by surveyors? _____

_____

What two measurements are needed to build a road?_____

_____

Why do surveyors measure the size of a lake? _____

Why do they map out the bottom of a lake? _____

Reading for Understanding

4. Place the correct letter in the blank.

_____ elevation   a. exact; definite; accurate

_____ "lay out"   b. art and science of measuring the land

_____ surveying   c. drawing that shows how much earth must be removed or added before construction begins

_____ property lines   d. procedure where a project is precisely measured and marked with wooden stakes

_____ precision   e. used so people know who owns a piece of land

Answer Key

Name _____

The Hollow Hills of Ireland

Main Idea
1. Choose another title for this story.

_____ Lammas Tide

_____ The Fairy King

__X__ An Irish Legend

Sequencing
2. Number the events below in the order that they happened.

_1_ The fairies lure human musicians inside.

_3_ Humans who are not careful eat the food.

_2_ The Sidhe offer visitors delicious-looking food.

_4_ Humans become servants and can never leave.

Reading for Details
3. Scan the story and answer the questions.

Who are the Sidhe? _fairies_

What do the Sidhe live in? _fairy palaces_

Where are the fairy palaces? _inside the magic hills_

When is Lammas Tide? What is it? _August 7; the night the fairies move from one hill to another_

Why won't a wise person try to climb the magic hills? _The fairies pinch and poke them._

Reading for Understanding
Many things in my world are magic. Check the one that is not.

_____ trees

_____ hills

__X__ gold

_____ palaces

_____ food

Since I do not have to work, I spend my time doing all of these things except

_____ dancing

_____ singing

_____ feasting

__X__ sleeping

_____ pinching

Name _____

When the Flowers Ran Away

Main Idea
1. This story explains

_____ why there are spirits on earth.

__X__ why flowers wither at the end of summer and come back in the spring.

_____ why bees could not make honey.

Sequencing
2. Number the events below in the order that they happened.

_3_ The people were unhappy without their flowers and asked Baiame for help.

_5_ The flowers withered at the end of the summer.

_4_ The men picked as many flowers as they could carry.

_2_ The flowers grew dissatisfied on earth and went to Pullima.

_1_ Baiame made the world and everything in it.

Reading for Details
3. Scan the story and answer the questions.

Who was Baiame? _the great spirit_

What things did Baiame make? _the world, animals, sky, sun, moon, stars_

Where did Baiame make his home? _in the sky_

Why did the flowers run away? _They wanted to be with Baiame._

When did the people notice the flowers were gone? _in the morning_

Reading for Understanding
4. Write the correct letter in the space.

_b_ Baiame   a. Baiame's home

_a_ Pullima   b. Great Spirit

_d_ wither   c. thriving and successful

_c_ prosperous   d. to fade away and die

Name _____

The Story of Babushka

Main Idea
1. This story explains

_____ why Babushka searches for the strangers and the Prince.

_____ why some people take journeys.

__X__ the Russian belief that children receive toys from an old woman while they sleep.

Sequencing
2. Number the events below in the order that they happened.

_2_ The men invited Babushka on their journey.

_3_ The strangers left without Babushka.

_1_ Three strangers knocked on Babushka's door.

_5_ Babushka searched for the strangers, leaving toys for good Russian children.

_4_ Babushka found some toys for the Prince.

Reading for Details
3. Scan the story and answer the questions.

Where did Babushka live? _Russia_

When did the strangers come to Babushka's door? _a winter night_

What did the strangers want? _for Babushka to bring a gift and come with them._

Why wouldn't Babushka go with them? _She was too poor and old._

Why did Babushka search for the strangers and the Prince? _She couldn't forget the men's faces, and she found a toy._

Reading for Understanding
4. Choose the best answer.

After the men left, Babushka felt

__X__ regretful   _____ forgetful   _____ confused

Babushka went out into the night with toys because she was

_____ thoughtless   __X__ hopeful   _____ crazy

Babushka continued looking for the men because she was

_____ dejected   _____ distracted   __X__ determined

Name _____

The Story of Kuma

Main Idea
1. This story tells about

_____ a man who took a ride in a big bowl.

__X__ a man who was greedy.

_____ a man who was a servant of the king.

Sequencing
2. Number the events below in the order that they happened.

_1_ Kuma was walking down the road complaining.

_3_ Nyamis gave Kuma two sacks.

_5_ Kuma untied the big sack and found stones.

_2_ Kuma was taken to see Nyamis.

_4_ Kuma gave the small sack to the king.

Reading for Details
3. Scan the story and answer the questions.

Who has a chief god named Nyamis? _Ashanti people of Africa_

What was Kuma always complaining about? _how hard he worked_

Where did Kuma meet the son of heaven? _on the road_

When was Kuma supposed to open the small sack? _after he gave the large one to the king_

Why did Kuma think he could give the small sack to the king? _because he thought no one knew he had two sacks_

Reading for Understanding
4. When an author tells what a character says, thinks, feels, or does, it helps you get to know the character. Check the things you learned about Kuma.

__X__ He was a complainer.

_____ He was happy.

__X__ He was a cheater.

__X__ He was greedy.

_____ He was a good listener.

Answer Key

Theseus and the Minotaur

Main Idea
1. This story tells
   ___ how Ariadne fell in love with Theseus.
   _X_ how Theseus freed Athens from the Minotaur.
   ___ how fourteen young people came to Crete.

Sequencing
2. Number the events below in the order that they happened.
   _5_ The people of Athens celebrated.
   _1_ Theseus offered to be King Minos' victim.
   _3_ Theseus defeated the Minotaur.
   _4_ Fourteen young people escaped from the Labyrinth.
   _2_ Ariadne fell in love with Theseus and offered to help him.

Reading for Details
3. Scan the story and answer the questions.
   Where did this story take place? _Greece_
   When did King Minos go to Athens? _every year_
   Why did he go? _to get seven maidens and seven youths to feed to the Minotaur_
   Why did Theseus take a ball of thread with him into the Labyrinth? _to find his way back out_
   Who celebrated the defeat of the Minotaur? _Athenians_

Reading for Understanding
4. Write the correct letter in the space.
   _d_ Minotaur   a. ruler of Crete
   _e_ Labyrinth   b. city in ancient Greece
   _a_ King Minos   c. maker of the Labyrinth
   _f_ Crete   d. beast
   _b_ Athens   e. maze
   _h_ Theseus   f. island in the center of the Labyrinth
   _g_ Ariadne   g. daughter of King Minos
   _c_ Daedalus   h. hero

Page 11

Beowulf, the Mighty Hero

Main Idea
1. This story tells how
   _X_ Beowulf saved Hrothgar and his people.
   ___ Grendel killed the soldiers.
   ___ perfect life was in England.

Sequencing
2. Number the events below in the order that they happened.
   _1_ Grendel killed many of Hrothgar's soldiers.
   _4_ Grendel fought Beowulf.
   _5_ Beowulf found Grendel dead.
   _3_ Beowulf set a trap for Grendel.
   _2_ Beowulf heard about Grendel's terrible deed.

Reading for Details
3. Scan the story and answer the questions.
   Who was Hrothgar? _the king of England_
   What did Hrothgar love to do? _to give feasts_
   Where did Grendel live? _in a nearby swamp_
   When did Hrothgar find most of his men dead? _in the morning_
   Why did Beowulf go to Hrothgar? _because he knew Hrothgar was a good king_

Reading for Understanding
4. Circle yes or no.
   I could have caught Grendel.   (Yes) No
   If Hrothgar gets into trouble again, I will save him.   (Yes) No
   If Hrothgar invites me to another feast, I will go.   (Yes) No

Page 13

Pyole and Krishna

Main Idea
1. Choose another title for this story.
   _X_ How a Call for Help was Answered
   ___ A Frightening Forest
   ___ A Blue Light

Sequencing
2. Number the events below in the order that they happened.
   _4_ Krishna walked through the forest with Pyole.
   _3_ His mother told Pyole to call on the god, Krishna, to walk through the forest with him.
   _1_ Pyole walked to school everyday through a huge and frightening forest.
   _2_ Pyole refused to go to school.
   _5_ Krishna refused to appear before Pyole's teacher.

Reading for Details
3. Scan the story and answer the questions.
   Who knows that the gods are always close by? _Hindu children of India_
   What hides behind the rocks in the forest? _wild animals_
   Where was the nearest school? _on the other side of the forest_
   When did Krishna walk through the forest with Pyole? _every evening after he called him_
   Why didn't Krishna let Pyole's teacher see him? _because he didn't need help_

Reading for Understanding
4. Place the descriptive word or phrase in the correct column.

huge and frightening, tall, wild animals and snakes, in a simple robe, tall trees, kind face, played a flute, very dark, animal voices and shining eyes, surrounded by blue light

Forest	Krishna
huge and frightening,	_tall,_
wild animals and snakes,	_in a simple robe,_
tall trees,	_kind face,_
very dark,	_played a flute,_
animal voices and	_surrounded by_
shining eyes	_blue light_

Page 15

The Greatest Oil Man

Main Idea
1. Choose another title for this story.
   ___ How to Start an Oil Well
   ___ A Texas Sandstorm
   _X_ A Tale about Kemp Morgan

Sequencing
2. Number the events below in order.
   _2_ He would dig with a shovel until he hit hard rock.
   _5_ Morgan would move on looking for more oil.
   _3_ Morgan would put up a derrick.
   _1_ Morgan would smell oil in the ground.
   _4_ He would drill for twenty-four hours a day until he struck oil.

Reading for Details
3. Scan the story and answer the questions.
   Who thought that Kemp Morgan was the greatest oil man of all? _the other oil drillers_
   What did Morgan sell to tire factories in Ohio? _ten foot pieces of rubber_
   When did Morgan discover that his mules were missing? _after he woke up_
   Where did Morgan find his mules after the sandstorm? _hanging from trees thirty feet in the air_
   Why didn't people know Kemp Morgan very well? _because he didn't talk much_

Reading for Understanding
4. Even though I don't talk much, people talk a lot about me.
   Check the one thing they do not say about me.
   ___ I work alone.
   ___ I can put up a derrick all by myself.
   ___ I run a drill twenty-four hours a day.
   _X_ I sometimes fall asleep while I'm drilling and then drill too deep.
   ___ I move around a lot.

Page 17

Answer Key

Name _____

The Singing Birds

Main Idea
1. This story is an Indian legend that explains
   _____ how the Great Spirit made many different animals.
   _____ why the Great Spirit was lonely in the winter.
   __X__ why the Great Spirit gave a voice to every bird.

Sequencing
2. Number the events below in the order that they happened.
   _1_ The Great Spirit made the world.
   _4_ The Great Spirit changed the falling leaves into birds.
   _2_ Because he was lonely, the Great Spirit made many animals.
   _5_ The birds stayed with the Great Spirit all winter.
   _3_ The animals hid away in the winter.
   _6_ The Great Spirit gave a voice to every bird.

Reading for Details
3. Scan the story and answer the questions.
   Who told this story? *American Indians*
   What colors were the birds? *yellow, red, brown*
   Where did the animals hide? *in holes and burrows*
   When did the Great Spirit smile? *when he saw the tiny, colorful birds*
   Why did the Great Spirit make the little birds? *so they would stay with him in the winter*

Reading for Understanding
4. Circle Yes or No.
   When all I could hear was the wind and the water, I was happy. — Yes (No)
   When I made the birds, I knew that I would no longer be lonely in the winter. — (Yes) No
   Even though the birds could not sing, I was completely happy. — Yes (No)
   When every bird had a voice, I was happy. — (Yes) No

Page 19

Name _____

John Henry, the Steel Driving Man

Main Idea
1. Choose another title for this story.
   _____ The Contest
   __X__ The Legend of John Henry
   _____ Steam Drill for Sale

Sequencing
2. Number the events below in the order that they happened.
   _4_ John Henry had drilled through sixteen feet of rock.
   _3_ A man showed up at the tunnel with a steam-powered drill for sale.
   _2_ John Henry got a job building railroad tunnels.
   _1_ John Henry was born a slave in Virginia.

Reading for Details
3. Scan the story to answer these questions.
   Who was born a slave? *John Henry*
   Where was John Henry born? *Virginia*
   What did John Henry do as a slave? *picked cotton and plowed fields*
   When was John Henry freed? *after the Civil War*
   Why did John Henry's boss think he didn't need the steam-powered drill? *because he knew how good John Henry was*

Reading for Understanding
4. Circle yes or no.
   People say that I am the biggest and scariest working man of all. — Yes (No)
   People say that I can swing my hammer higher and faster than anyone else. — (Yes) No
   People come from far away to watch me drive my sixteen pound hammer head into the rock. — (Yes) No
   People say that they can still hear my hammer ring early in the morning. — (Yes) No

Page 21

Name _____

The Building of the Round Table

Main Idea
1. Choose another title for this story.
   __X__ A New Table for King Arthur's Knights
   _____ King Arthur and his Knights
   _____ A Mystery Man

Sequencing
2. Number the events below in the order that they happened.
   _4_ The old man built a round table.
   _1_ A quarrel broke out among the knights.
   _5_ The knights sat around the table as equals.
   _3_ King Arthur declared that anyone who fought would be put to death.
   _2_ Soon the quarrel became a fight.

Reading for Details
3. Scan the story to answer these questions.
   Where did King Arthur and his knights live? *Camelot in England*
   What stood in the middle of the Great Hall of Arthur's castle? *great long table*
   Why did that table cause trouble? *A few knights insisted on the first seat*
   Who helped solve the problem in Camelot? *an old man*
   When did peace return to Camelot? *when the old man built the round table*

Reading for Understanding
4. Put each descriptive word in the correct column. Not all the words will be used.

magic, wise, brave, strange, beautiful, good, noble, common, round, long

Camelot	King Arthur	Knights
magic	*wise*	*brave*
beautiful	*good*	*noble*

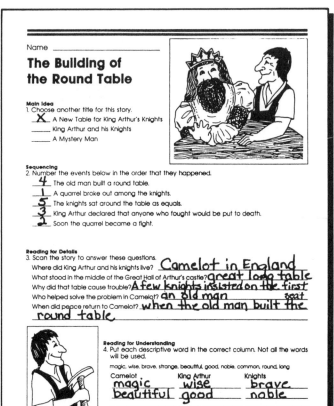

Page 23

Name _____

Bellerophon and Pegasus

Main Idea
1. This story explains
   __X__ the friendship of Pegasus and Bellerophon.
   _____ Bellerophon's dream.
   _____ the battle with the Chimaera.

Sequencing
2. Number the events below in the order that they happened.
   _2_ Bellerophon and Pegasus had a battle with the Chimaera.
   _3_ Bellerophon tried to ride Pegasus to Mount Olympus.
   _1_ Bellerophon and Pegasus became great friends.
   _5_ Pegasus served Zeus forever afterwards.
   _4_ Pegasus sadly threw Bellerophon off his back.

Reading for Details
3. Scan the story to answer these questions.
   Who was the only person able to capture Pegasus? *Bellerophon*
   What did Bellerophon use to capture Pegasus? *a golden bridle*
   When did Bellerophon find the bridle? *when he awoke*
   Where did Bellerophon and Pegasus travel together? *all over the world*
   Why did Pegasus throw Bellerophon off his back? *because he knew that Bellerophon could never enter Olympus*

Reading for Understanding
4. Place the correct letter in the blank.
   _c_ Pegasus   a. young Greek man
   _a_ Bellerophon   b. god
   _d_ Polydius   c. winged horse
   _e_ Athena   d. wise man
   _f_ Chimaera   e. goddess
   _g_ Mt. Olympus   f. beast
   _b_ Zeus   g. home of the gods

Page 25

The Extra Days of the Year

Name _____

Main Idea
1. Long ago people made up myths to explain why things happened. This myth explains
_____ why Ra became the sun-god.
_____ why Nut could not have any children.
__X__ why a year has 365 days and the moon grows smaller every month.

Sequencing
2. Number the events below in the order that they happened.
__3__ Thoth challenged Konsu to a game of checkers.
__4__ Thoth won enough moonlight to make five extra days.
__1__ Ra put a curse on Nut.
__5__ Nut had five children.
__2__ Nut asked Thoth for help.

Reading for Details
3. Scan the story to answer these questions.
Who was Ra? _the most loved ancient Egyptian god_
What was the curse that Ra put on Nut? _She could not bear a child on any day of the year._
Where did Thoth put the five extra days? _between the end of one year and the beginning of the new year_
When did Nut have her children? _over the years on one of the holidays_
Why was Ra forced to leave the earth? _because Osiris destroyed his body_

Reading for Understanding
4. Place the correct letter in the blank.
_c_ Ra   a. Nut's brother
_e_ Nut   b. Nut's child
_d_ Thoth   c. Sun-god
_d_ Konsu   d. Moon-god
_b_ Osiris   e. Ra's daughter

Page 27

Li Ching and the Rain Makers

Name _____

Main Idea
1. This story explains
_____ how the dragon rain makers could not make rain.
__X__ how Li Ching helped make the rain that ended the long drought.
_____ how Li Ching lost his way.

Sequencing
2. Number the events below in the order that they happened.
__3__ Li Ching rode the horse all night long making the rain.
__5__ His friends ran to meet him and told him about the great rain.
__1__ Li Ching went hunting and got lost.
__4__ Li Ching was given a bag of pearls for his help and shown the way home.
__2__ He found a grand palace.

Reading for Details
3. Scan the story to answer these questions.
Who tells the legend about the dragon gods? _Chinese_
What did the woman ask Li Ching to do? _help make rain_
Where was Li Ching instructed to put the drop of water? _on the horse's mane_
When did Li Ching return to the palace? _in the morning_
Why didn't the woman's sons make the rain? _They couldn't return from their travels in time._

Reading for Understanding
4. Place the letter in the correct blank.
_c_ Li Ching   a. made the sky, earth, people, and animals
_a_ Dragon-gods   b. no rainfall for a long time
_b_ drought   c. a great scholar
_d_ vanish   d. to disappear

Page 29

The Flying Dutchman

Name _____

Main Idea
1. This story tells
_____ about a robbery at sea.
__X__ why a ghost ship sails near the Cape of Good Hope.
_____ about a rich Dutchman.

Sequencing
2. Number the events below in the order that they happened.
__2__ The captain and the rich passenger talked about their riches.
__5__ The ship tried unsuccessfully to reach the shore.
__1__ The Flying Dutchman was sailing back to the Netherlands.
__3__ The crew tied up the captain and the passenger and threw them overboard.
__4__ A mysterious plague broke out among the crew.

Reading for Details
3. Scan the story to answer these questions.
Who tells the sea stories? _sailors_
What is the Flying Dutchman? _the ship that freezes the hearts of sailors_
Where was the ship sailing to? _the Netherlands_
When did the crew tie up the captain and the passenger and throw them overboard? _after they found their money_
Why do sailors near the Cape of Good Hope keep their fingers crossed? _hoping they will not see the Flying Dutchman_

Reading for Understanding
4. Circle yes or no.
I say that the Flying Dutchman is still haunting the Cape of Good Hope.   (Yes)   No
My story begins when the ship was sailing back to the islands off India.   Yes   (No)
After we got rid of the captain and the passenger, we headed for the nearest port.   (Yes)   No
I got sick and was very thirsty, but I saw a doctor when I reached port.   Yes   (No)

Page 31

How Cuchulainn Got his Name

Name _____

Main Idea
1. Choose another title for this story.
_____ A New Name for Setanta
__X__ Cuchulainn's First Adventure
_____ An Unusual Watchdog

Sequencing
2. Number the events below in the order that they happened.
__3__ Setanta arrived at Culann's house later.
__5__ Setanta promised to guard the house until a new dog was trained.
__4__ Setanta killed Culann's hound.
__2__ The king arrived first at Culann's house.
__1__ The king asked Setanta to go to a banquet at the blacksmith's house.
__6__ Setanta was given the name Cuchulainn.

Reading for Details
3. Scan the story to answer these questions.
Where did this story take place? _Ireland_
Who told Setanta's mother that her baby would become a great hero? _a god_
What was special about Setanta as he was growing? _He was the strongest boy at the king's palace_
When did Culann let his dog out into the yard? _When the king and his warriors arrived_
Why was Culann angry with Setanta? _because he killed his dog_

Reading for Understanding
4. Choose another solution to each of Setanta's problems.
When the dog rushed at Setanta, he could have
__X__ stuffed the ball into the dog's mouth and then ran into the house.
_____ ran up a tree.
_____ thrown the ball and played a game with the dog.
When Culann was angry at Setanta and demanded payment, Setanta could have
__X__ given him money to buy and train a new dog.
_____ told him that he was simply defending himself and owed him nothing.
_____ borrowed another dog.

Page 33

Atalanta and the Golden Apples

Name _____

Main Idea
1. Choose another title for this story.
_____ The Race
__X__ How Melanion Outsmarted Atalanta
_____ The Fastest Runner

Sequencing
2. Number the events below in the order that they happened.
_2_ Kindly hunters adopted Atalanta.
_5_ Melanion won by dropping the golden apples.
_1_ Atalanta's father left her on a mountainside.
_4_ Melanion challenged Atalanta to a race.
_6_ Atalanta married Melanion.
_3_ Atalanta announced she would marry the first man who could beat her in a foot race.

Reading for Details
3. Scan the story to answer these questions.
Who nursed Atalanta and raised her? _a bear_
What plan did Atalanta think of to avoid marriage? _She would marry the first man who beat her in a foot race._
Where did Melanion get the three golden apples? _from the end of the world_
When did Atalanta sprint like the wind? _when she saw Melanion ahead of her_
Why did Atalanta marry Melanion? _because she admired him_

Reading for Understanding
4. Check the correct answer(s).
I became a fast runner because
_____ I didn't weigh much.
__X__ I was strong.
__X__ I was raised in the wild.
I avoided marriage because
__X__ I was happy with my life.
_____ I didn't like men.
_____ I was waiting for a bear.
I married Melanion because
__X__ I said I would.
_____ I liked him.
__X__ I admired his cleverness.

Thor Recovers his Stolen Hammer

Name _____

Main Idea
1. Choose another title for this story.
_____ A Trip to Giantland
_____ The Mysterious Bride
__X__ Thor's Magic Hammer

Sequencing
2. Number the events below in the order that they happened.
_1_ Loki had a plan to get Thor's hammer back.
_5_ Thor swung the hammer and brought down the walls of the castle.
_3_ Thor and Loki arrived at Thrym's castle.
_2_ Thor dressed up as a bride for Thrym.
_4_ Thrym had Thor's hammer brought in.
_6_ Thor went home peacefully.

Reading for Details
3. Scan the story to answer these questions.
Who ordered Loki to go to Giantland? _Thor_
What caused the terrible storm in Giantland? _Thor's hammer_
Where was Thrym swinging the hammer? _On the mountain top_
When was Thor sick with anger? _when he heard Thrym's demand to have Freya as his bride_
Why did Thor wear a veil? _to hide his great flowing beard_

Reading for Understanding
4. Choose the correct word in each sentence below.
When I found out that the Giants had my hammer, I was (furious, calm).
When I heard that Thrym wanted to trade my hammer for Freya, I was (angry, amused).
When I was dressed up as a bride, I was (excited, unhappy).
When I roared at Thrym and brought down the castle walls with my hammer, I was (sad, triumphant).
When I went back home with my hammer, I was (peaceful, agitated).

Bloodstoppers

Name _____

Main Idea
1. This story explains
_____ how Tom's cousin cut his arm.
_____ Tom's long ride in the wagon.
__X__ a bloodstopper's special power.

Sequencing
2. Number the events below in the order that they happened.
_4_ Tom started out to get a doctor.
_6_ Tom went back to the farmhouse to find his cousin's arm had stopped bleeding.
_1_ Tom and his cousin were cutting hay.
_2_ Tom's cousin cut his arm with a scythe.
_5_ Tom met Ben, a bloodstopper.
_3_ Tom and his cousin walked back home.

Reading for Details
3. Scan the story to answer these questions.
What special power does a bloodstopper have? _to stop bleeding with the touch of a hand or by saying special words or prayers_
Where was Tom going when he met Ben? _to get a doctor_
Why did Ben tell Tom to go back home? _His cousin had stopped bleeding._
Why do some people believe in bloodstoppers? _They think they have been cured by one._
Who can be a bloodstopper? _7th sons of 7th sons; 7th daughters of 7th daughters_

Reading for Understanding
4. Circle yes or no.
People say I have mysterious healing powers. (Yes) No
People say I can make a person bleed by touching him/her or by saying special words or prayers. Yes (No)
People say I am a bloodstopper because I am the seventh son of my father who is the seventh son. (Yes) No
People say they believe in me because I can cure them. (Yes) No

---

The Rarest Bird

Name _____

Main Idea
1. Choose another title for this story.
_____ Building an Expressway
_____ Spraying DDT
__X__ Destroying the "Duskies"

Sequencing
2. Number the events below in the order that they happened.
_1_ DDT spray decreased the sparrow population by 75 per cent.
_5_ Only four male duskies were left.
_2_ The sparrows' nesting grounds were destroyed by flooding.
_4_ People moving into that area destroyed the sparrows' home, destroying even more of the duskies.
_3_ Nine hundred more pairs of sparrows were found in an unexplored area.

Reading for Details
3. Scan the story to answer these questions.
Where do the dusky seaside sparrows live? _St. John River area in Florida_
When did their problems begin? _as people began moving into the area_
Why was DDT sprayed in the area? _to kill mosquitoes_
Who is trying to help the duskies today? _ornithologists from Walt Disney Discovery Island_
What are they trying to do? _Cross breed the male duskies with female sparrows that look similar_

Reading for Understanding
4. Place the correct letter in the blank.
_c_ DDT   a. scientists who study birds
_a_ ornithologists b. sparrows living in tidal marshes
_b_ "duskies"   c. a poison used to kill mosquitoes
_d_ crossbreed   d. to produce an offspring from a male and female of different breeds

Euglena, the Mystery Creature

Main Idea
1. This story tells about
___ chlorophyll in plants.
_X_ an organism that seems to be both a plant and an animal.
___ the plant kingdom and the animal kingdom.

Sequencing
2. Number the events below in the order that they happened.
_3_ Scientists found that the Euglena had characteristics of both the plant and animal kingdom.
_2_ They separated plants and animals into two kingdoms.
_1_ Scientists began studying the world of living things.
_4_ The Euglena remains a mysterious creature to scientists.

Reading for Details
3. Scan the story to answer these questions.
What kind of scientists study the Euglena? **biologists**
Why are they puzzled by this creature? **because it has characteristics of both plants and animals**
What plant-like characteristics does the Euglena have? **It has chlorophyll.**
What animal-like characteristics does the Euglena have? **mouth, gullet, swims, eye which can detect light**
Where does the Euglena live? **in ponds and swamps**

Reading for Understanding
4. Place the correct letter in the blank.
_f_ animal kingdom a. scientists who study living things
_b_ plant kingdom b. members cannot move very much on their own
_e_ flagellum c. gives plants their green color
_c_ chlorophyll d. one-celled animals
_a_ biologists e. a long tail
_g_ algae f. members move from place to place by themselves
_d_ protozoa g. one-celled plants

The Simplest Machines

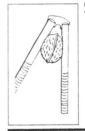

Main Idea
1. Choose another title for this story.
___ The Seesaw
___ When Your Arm Becomes a Lever
_X_ An Old and Useful Tool

Sequencing
2. Number the events below in the order necessary to explain how a lever works
_4_ The weight and the force are connected by the arm.
_1_ A lever is made up of four parts that work together.
_3_ The force moves the weight.
_2_ The parts are the force, the weight, the arm, and the fulcrum.
_5_ The force, the weight, and the arm rest on the fulcrum.

Reading for Details
3. Scan the story to answer these questions.
Why are levers useful today? **because they make up most of the simple tools that we use**
What is a good example of a lever with the fulcrum between the force and the weight? **seesaw**
Where is the person on the seesaw when he is the weight? **in the air**
When does he become the force? **when he is on the ground**
How can levers be made to do different kinds of work? **The four parts can be placed in different positions.**

Reading for Understanding
4. Place these tools in the correct column.
knife, rake, scissors, lathe, wheelbarrow, screwdriver, nutcracker, crowbar, drill, egg beater, wagon, broom, bottle opener, saw, hammer, windmill.

Levers	Non-levers
scissors	knife
broom	screwdriver
rake	drill
wheelbarrow	egg beater
nutcracker	wagon
crowbar	saw
bottle opener	windmill
hammer	lathe

The Unusual Behavior of Floating Ice

Main Idea
1. This story explains
_X_ why ice is able to float.
___ what happens when things get colder.
___ why you shouldn't put a bottle of soda pop in the freezer.

Sequencing
2. Number the events below in the order that they happen.
_4_ The liquid gets heavier.
_5_ When the liquid gets cold enough, it freezes.
_2_ The molecules get closer together.
_1_ The liquid cools.
_3_ More molecules fit into the same space.

Reading for Details
3. Scan the story to answer these questions.
How is water different than other liquids? **It expands instead of contracting when it freezes.**
Why is ice able to float? **It is lighter than the liquid.**
When is expanding ice helpful? **in lakes, streams, drinks**
When is it harmful? **when it gets into cracks in streets**
What would happen if ice sank in lakes and rivers? **It would kill the plants and animals.**

Reading for Understanding
4. Circle yes or no.

Water is heavier in its frozen form than in its liquid form. Yes **No**
As it cools, water gets heavier and heavier. **Yes** No
Water is heaviest at 34° Farenheit or 1° Celsius. **Yes** No
As it freezes, water suddenly explodes and floats away. Yes **No**

The Story of Color

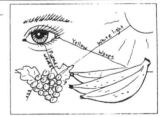

Main Idea
1. Choose another title for this story.
___ The Colors of the Rainbow
___ Raindrops and Other Prisms
_X_ Light and Color

Sequencing
2. Number the events below in the order that they happen.
_3_ The rest of the light is reflected.
_1_ White light shines on an object.
_2_ The object absorbs some of the light.
_4_ Your eyes see the reflected light.

Reading for Details
3. Scan the story to answer these questions.
What seven colors is light made of? **red, orange, yellow, green, blue, indigo, violet**
Why does light usually look white? **the different waves travel in different directions and mix together**
When do we see color? **when an object reflects a colored light**
Where does the colored light reflect? **back to our eyes**
Why don't we see color at night? **not enough light to reflect into our eyes**

Reading for Understanding
4. Place the correct letter in the blank.

_c_ light a. color of the light wave it reflects
_d_ colors b. special piece of glass which separates light into seven colors
_b_ prism c. made up of seven kinds of waves
_e_ absorb d. different kinds of light waves
_g_ reflect e. soak up
_a_ color of object f. sunlight separated into colors by raindrops
_f_ rainbow g. bounce back

Answer Key

A, B, and O: The Blood Group Alphabet

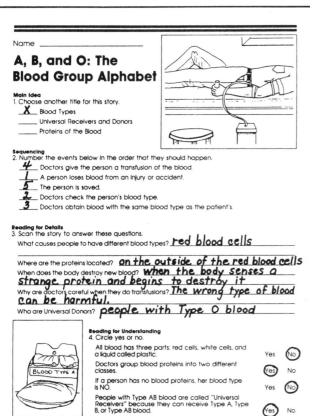

Main Idea
1. Choose another title for this story.
   - **X** Blood Types
   - _____ Universal Receivers and Donors
   - _____ Proteins of the Blood

Sequencing
2. Number the events below in the order that they should happen.
   - **4** Doctors give the person a transfusion of the blood.
   - **1** A person loses blood from an injury or accident.
   - **5** The person is saved.
   - **2** Doctors check the person's blood type.
   - **3** Doctors obtain blood with the same blood type as the patient's.

Reading for Details
3. Scan the story to answer these questions.
   What causes people to have different blood types? _red blood cells_

   Where are the proteins located? _on the outside of the red blood cells_
   When does the body destroy new blood? _when the body senses a strange protein and begins to destroy it_
   Why are doctors careful when they do transfusions? _The wrong type of blood can be harmful._
   Who are Universal Donors? _people with Type O blood_

Reading for Understanding
4. Circle yes or no.
   - All blood has three parts: red cells, white cells, and a liquid called plastic. — Yes **No**
   - Doctors group blood proteins into two different classes. — **Yes** No
   - If a person has no blood proteins, her blood type is NO. — Yes **No**
   - People with Type AB blood are called "Universal Receivers" because they can receive Type A, Type B, or Type AB blood. — **Yes** No

Page 51

Earthquakes— Nature at Work

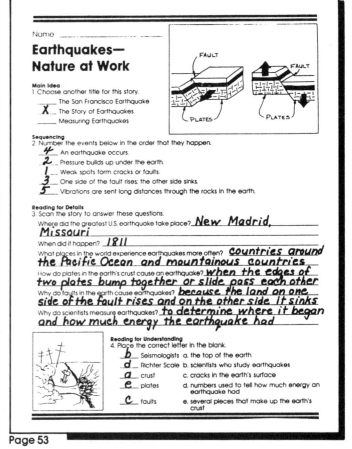

Main Idea
1. Choose another title for this story.
   - _____ The San Francisco Earthquake
   - **X** The Story of Earthquakes
   - _____ Measuring Earthquakes

Sequencing
2. Number the events below in the order that they happen.
   - **4** An earthquake occurs.
   - **2** Pressure builds up under the earth.
   - **1** Weak spots form cracks or faults.
   - **3** One side of the fault rises; the other side sinks.
   - **5** Vibrations are sent long distances through the rocks in the earth.

Reading for Details
3. Scan the story to answer these questions.
   Where did the greatest U.S. earthquake take place? _New Madrid, Missouri_
   When did it happen? _1811_
   What places in the world experience earthquakes more often? _countries around the Pacific Ocean and mountainous countries_
   How do plates in the earth's crust cause an earthquake? _when the edges of two plates bump together or slide pass each other_
   Why do faults in the earth cause earthquakes? _because the land on one side of the fault rises and on the other side it sinks_
   Why do scientists measure earthquakes? _to determine where it began and how much energy the earthquake had_

Reading for Understanding
4. Place the correct letter in the blank.
   - **b** Seismologists — a. the top of the earth
   - **d** Richter Scale — b. scientists who study earthquakes
   - **a** crust — c. cracks in the earth's surface
   - **e** plates — d. numbers used to tell how much energy an earthquake had
   - **c** faults — e. several pieces that make up the earth's crust

Page 53

Accidents, Dreams, and Discoveries

Main Idea
1. This story explains
   - _____ how Isaac Newton discovered the third law of gravity.
   - _____ how flies walk on ceilings.
   - **X** how important discoveries are sometimes made during relaxation.

Sequencing
2. Number the events below in the order that they happened.
   - **5** Isaac Newton developed the third law of gravity.
   - **2** Isaac Newton sat under an apple tree.
   - **1** Newton took the day off from work to relax.
   - **3** An apple fell to the ground.
   - **4** The apple gave him the clue that he needed.

Reading for Details
3. Scan the story to answer these questions.
   Who invented the sewing machine? _Elias Howe_
   Why had Howe given up and gone to sleep? _long day of failure_

   What helped Howe solve his problem? _a dream_

   Where were the holes in the spears that Howe dreamed about? _in their points_

   When did Howe's invention finally work? _when he put the eye of the sewing machine needle at the pointed end_

Reading for Understanding
4. Circle yes or no.
   - I invented a perfect way to make pictures of mathematical equations on graph paper. — **Yes** No
   - A fly helped me. — **Yes** No
   - I swatted the fly. — Yes **No**
   - My method is outdated today. — Yes **No**

Page 55

The Pest That Can Save Lives

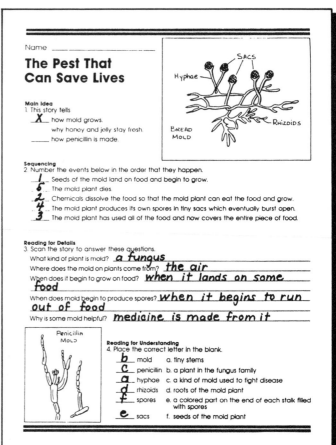

Main Idea
1. This story tells
   - **X** how mold grows.
   - _____ why honey and jelly stay fresh.
   - _____ how penicillin is made.

Sequencing
2. Number the events below in the order that they happen.
   - **1** Seeds of the mold land on food and begin to grow.
   - **6** The mold plant dies.
   - **2** Chemicals dissolve the food so that the mold plant can eat the food and grow.
   - **4** The mold plant produces its own spores in tiny sacs which eventually burst open.
   - **3** The mold plant has used all of the food and now covers the entire piece of food.

Reading for Details
3. Scan the story to answer these questions.
   What kind of plant is mold? _a fungus_
   Where does the mold on plants come from? _the air_
   When does it begin to grow on food? _when it lands on some food_
   When does mold begin to produce spores? _when it begins to run out of food_
   Why is some mold helpful? _medicine is made from it_

Reading for Understanding
4. Place the correct letter in the blank.
   - **b** mold — a. tiny stems
   - **c** penicillin — b. a plant in the fungus family
   - **a** hyphae — c. a kind of mold used to fight disease
   - **d** rhizoids — d. roots of the mold plant
   - **f** spores — e. a colored part on the end of each stalk filled with spores
   - **e** sacs — f. seeds of the mold plant

Page 57

Answer Key

The Duckbilled Platypus: Nature's Experiment

Main Idea
1. This story tells about
   X a rare and unusual animal.
   ____ the family of the very first mammals.
   ____ a special nose.

Sequencing
2. Number the events below in the order that they happen.
   2 The female platypus lays her eggs.
   1 The female platypus builds a burrow lined with grass and leaves.
   5 The mother teaches her babies to swim.
   3 The platypus curls up around the eggs to keep them warm.
   4 The eggs hatch.

Reading for Details
3. Scan the story and answer these questions.
   Where does the platypus live? *Eastern Australia*
   Why is a platypus only seen in Australia? *It dies in captivity.*
   What does the body of the platypus look like? *a beaver*
   When does a platypus go swimming? *at night*
   Why does the platypus keep the end of its bill out of the water as it swims? *to breathe*

Reading for Understanding
4. I am called "Nature's Experiment" because I am a mammal with characteristics of birds and reptiles. List my characteristics in the correct column.

body like a beaver, swims, has a bill, has webbed feet, breathes with lungs, furry, lays eggs, feeds young with own milk, body temperature same as surrounding temperature

Mammal	Reptile	Bird
body like a beaver; furry; food from mother's milk; lungs and breathes air	*swims; body temperature same as surrounding temperature*	*has a bill; has webbed feet; lays eggs*

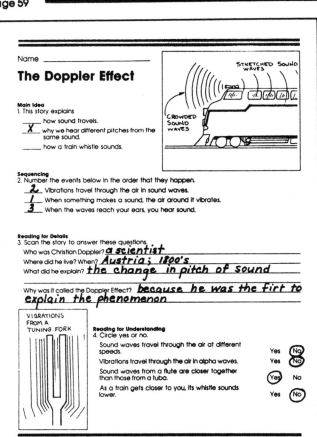

Page 59

The Whooping Crane, A Bird in Danger

Main Idea
1. This story tells about
   ____ the yearly migration of the whooping crane.
   X the plight of the whooping crane.
   ____ foster parents for the whooping crane.

Sequencing
2. Number the events below in the order that they happened.
   3 Conservationists became concerned about the whooping crane.
   1 Hunters shot many whooping cranes.
   4 The U.S. Congress declared the whooping crane an endangered species.
   2 Fewer than two dozen whooping cranes were left.
   5 It became a crime to kill whooping cranes.

Reading for Details
3. Scan the story to answer these questions.
   Why is it a crime to kill the whooping crane? *because it is an endangered species*
   What danger threatens the whooping crane? *extinction*
   Who is trying to help the whooping crane? *biologists and birdwatchers*
   Where do biologists put some of the whooping crane's eggs? *in sandhill cranes' nests*
   Why do they do this? *so more whooping cranes will survive*

Reading for Understanding
4. Circle yes or no.

The whooping crane is a large, pink bird.	Yes	**No**
It has red wing tips and a black face.	Yes	**No**
It stands four feet tall, has a long neck, and long legs.	**Yes**	No
The whooping crane's neck helps it see great distances.	**Yes**	No
Its wings measure seven feet across when they're spread out.	**Yes**	No

Page 61

The Doppler Effect

Main Idea
1. This story explains
   ____ how sound travels.
   X why we hear different pitches from the same sound.
   ____ how a train whistle sounds.

Sequencing
2. Number the events below in the order that they happen.
   2 Vibrations travel through the air in sound waves.
   1 When something makes a sound, the air around it vibrates.
   3 When the waves reach your ears, you hear sound.

Reading for Details
3. Scan the story to answer these questions.
   Who was Christian Doppler? *a scientist*
   Where did he live? When? *Austria; 1800's*
   What did he explain? *the change in pitch of sound*

   Why was it called the Doppler Effect? *because he was the first to explain the phenomenon*

Reading for Understanding
4. Circle yes or no.

Sound waves travel through the air at different speeds.	Yes	**No**
Vibrations travel through the air in alpha waves.	Yes	**No**
Sound waves from a flute are closer together than those from a tuba.	**Yes**	No
As a train gets closer to you, its whistle sounds lower.	Yes	**No**

Page 63

The Great Fire Mystery

Main Idea
1. This story explains
   ____ how to store materials safely.
   ____ flash fires and explosions.
   X spontaneous combustion.

Sequencing
2. Number the events below in the order that they happen.
   1 Oily rags are packed tightly into a box.
   3 Faster oxidation produces even more heat.
   4 Spontaneous combustion occurs.
   2 Heat builds up inside the box.

Reading for Details
3. Scan the story to answer these questions.
   What materials are most likely to produce spontaneous combustion? Why? *those that are damp and oily; oxidize faster*
   What causes fire? *heat that is given off when oxygen combines with some material*
   What is oxidation? *the combining of oxygen with a material*
   Why are powders dangerous? *oxygen combines with them quickly and produces heat quickly*
   How can spontaneous combustion be prevented? *Rags and papers should be stored dry and loose.*

Reading for Understanding
4. Place the correct letter in the blank.
   b oxygen combining with some material
   a gives off no light and very little heat
   d gives off much heat and light
   c when materials get so hot they explode into flames

   a. slow oxidation
   b. oxidation
   c. spontaneous combustion
   d. fast oxidation

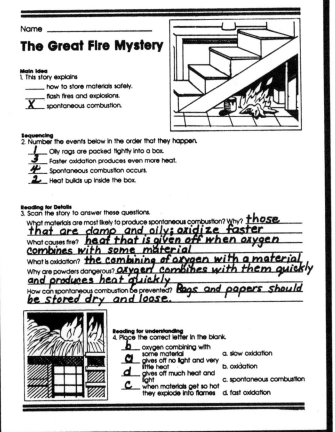

Page 65

Answer Key

The Rain that Kills

Main Idea
1. This story tells about
_____ the water cycle.
__X__ acid rain and the problems it causes.
_____ scientists learning about acid rain.

Sequencing
2. Number the events below in the order that they happen.
__2__ Gases and water droplets combine to form strong acids.
__4__ The acid rain corrodes metal and damages buildings.
__1__ Factories and automobiles give off gases.
__3__ Acids mix with water droplets and become acid rain or snow.

Reading for Details
3. Scan the story to answer these questions.
Why do plants need rain? *to make food and grow*
When can rain be harmful to plants? *when it is acid rain*
What areas are beginning to show severe damage? *forests around the world*
Who thinks that this damage is caused by acid rain? *scientists*
Why haven't we been able to stop the damage? *They are still learning about acid rain.*

Reading for Understanding
4. Place the correct letter in the blank.
__c__ sulfur dioxide   a. form clouds
__d__ environment   b. cannot live in very acidic water
__a__ water droplets   c. gas given off by cars and factories
__b__ fish   d. surroundings
__e__ acid rain   e. dangerous gases and rain drops mixed together

Page 67

Shifting Continents

Main Idea
1. Choose another title for this story.
_____ The Earth's Crust
_____ The Earth–A Big Jigsaw Puzzle
__X__ The Continental Drift Theory

Sequencing
2. Number the events below in the order that they happened.
__4__ The two large pieces gradually broke up into the continents of today.
__5__ Movement of magma carried the continents away from each other.
__1__ The continents were joined into a huge land mass.
__3__ Pangaea broke into two pieces.
__2__ Magma rose up through the ocean and formed new crust.

Reading for Details
3. Scan the story to answer these questions.
Who developed the Continental Drift theory? *Alfred Wegener*
What evidence is there that the continents were once connected? *rock structures, fossils*
When do geologists think that all the continents were connected? *millions of years ago*
What continents made up one of the two pieces of broken Pangaea? *Europe, Asia, N. America; Africa, S. America, Australia, Antarica*
When do geologists predict that the Atlantic Ocean will be wider than it is today? *50 million years from now*

Reading for Understanding
4. Place the correct letter in the blank.
__c__ Pangaea   a. theory that explains why there are seven continents instead of one
__a__ Continental Drift   b. ancient remains of plants and animals
__b__ fossils   c. name of huge land mass formed by all the continents
__f__ crust   d. thick liquid of melted rock
__d__ magma   e. scientists who study the earth
__e__ geologists   f. top layer of the earth

Page 69

The Hungry Brain

Main Idea
1. This story explains
__X__ how the brain controls hunger feelings.
_____ that rats are used for scientific experiments.
_____ why blood runs through the brain.

Sequencing
2. Number the events below in the order that they happen.
__1__ Blood vessels in the hypothalamus don't have enough nutrients.
__4__ The animal or person feels hungry.
__3__ The hypothalamus sends signals to the stomach to start churning.
__2__ The hypothalamus senses that the body will soon run out of energy.
__5__ The hypothalamus stops sending signals when the blood has enough nutrients.

Reading for Details
3. Scan the story to answer these questions.
What part of the brain controls hunger? *the hypothalamus*
What did scientists use to study hunger feelings? *a rat and an electric wire*
Where did scientists put the thin wire? *In the rat's hypothalamus*
When would the rat eat even though its stomach was full? *when the rat received an electric current in a part of the brain*
Why would the hungry rat refuse to eat? *when the scientists moved the wire to a different part of the hypothalamus*

Reading for Understanding
4. Choose the topic for each paragraph.
Paragraph 2
__X__ Experiments with rats helped scientists learn about hunger feelings.
_____ Electric currents are used in experiments with rats.
_____ Rats are not hurt in scientific experiments.
Paragraph 3
_____ People don't have wires in their brains.
_____ A quiet stomach is a full stomach.
__X__ Several parts of the body are involved in sensing hunger.

Page 71

The Mighty Virus

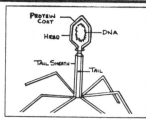

Main Idea
1. This story tells about
__X__ viruses.
_____ chemical crystals.
_____ DNA and RNA.

Sequencing
2. Number the events below in the order that they happen.
__5__ The plant or animal the virus has attacked becomes sick.
__1__ A virus meets a living cell.
__4__ The cell produces more viruses just like the invading virus.
__3__ The virus' DNA combines with the cell's DNA.
__2__ The protein coat pushes the virus' DNA into a cell.

Reading for Details
3. Scan the story to answer these questions.
What is a virus made of? *core of DNA or RNA and a coating of protein*
What does DNA and RNA do for a virus? *They help it reproduce.*
When does a virus come alive? *when it meets a living cell*
What are two ways to fight viruses? *vaccinations and rest*
Why is it lucky that most viruses die quickly? *There is no cure for viral infections.*

Reading for Understanding
4. Place the correct letter in the blank.
__c__ protein coat   a. state of a virus outside of a living plant or animal
__d__ tomatoes   b. weak virus given to people to prevent diseases
__b__ vaccination   c. pushes the virus' DNA into a living cell
__a__ chemical crystal d. can be destroyed by viral disease

Page 73

Answer Key

pH—The Chemist's Tool

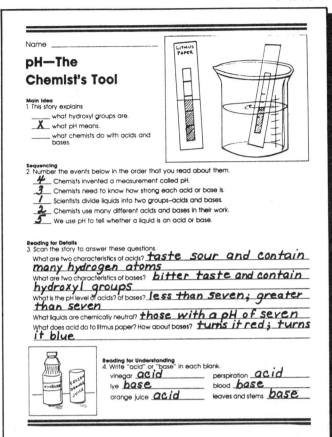

Main Idea
1. This story explains
   _____ what hydroxyl groups are.
   __X__ what pH means.
   _____ what chemists do with acids and bases.

Sequencing
2. Number the events below in the order that you read about them.
   _4_ Chemists invented a measurement called pH.
   _3_ Chemists need to know how strong each acid or base is.
   _1_ Scientists divide liquids into two groups–acids and bases.
   _2_ Chemists use many different acids and bases in their work.
   _5_ We use pH to tell whether a liquid is an acid or base.

Reading for Details
3. Scan the story to answer these questions.
   What are two characteristics of acids? _taste sour and contain many hydrogen atoms_
   What are two characteristics of bases? _bitter taste and contain hydroxyl groups_
   What is the pH level of acids? of bases? _less than seven; greater than seven_
   What liquids are chemically neutral? _those with a pH of seven_
   What does acid do to litmus paper? How about bases? _turns it red; turns it blue_

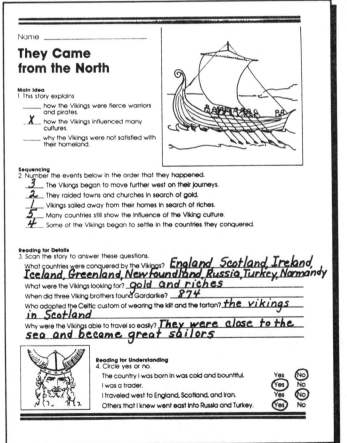

Reading for Understanding
4. Write "acid" or "base" in each blank.
   vinegar _acid_   perspiration _acid_
   lye _base_   blood _base_
   orange juice _acid_   leaves and stems _base_

Page 75

Your Body's Fright Reaction

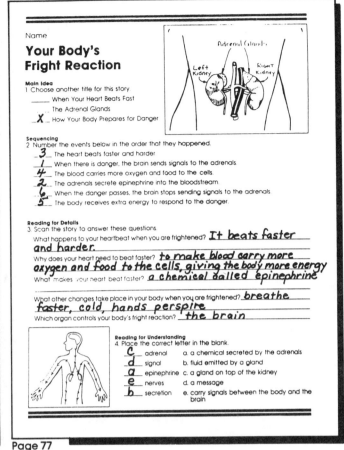

Main Idea
1. Choose another title for this story.
   _____ When Your Heart Beats Fast
   _____ The Adrenal Glands
   __X__ How Your Body Prepares for Danger

Sequencing
2. Number the events below in the order that they happened.
   _3_ The heart beats faster and harder.
   _1_ When there is danger, the brain sends signals to the adrenals.
   _4_ The blood carries more oxygen and food to the cells.
   _2_ The adrenals secrete epinephrine into the bloodstream.
   _6_ When the danger passes, the brain stops sending signals to the adrenals.
   _5_ The body receives extra energy to respond to the danger.

Reading for Details
3. Scan the story to answer these questions.
   What happens to your heartbeat when you are frightened? _It beats faster and harder._
   Why does your heart need to beat faster? _to make blood carry more oxygen and food to the cells, giving the body more energy_
   What makes your heart beat faster? _a chemical called epinephrine_
   What other changes take place in your body when you are frightened? _breathe faster, cold, hands perspire_
   Which organ controls your body's fright reaction? _the brain_

Reading for Understanding
4. Place the correct letter in the blank.
   _c_ adrenal   a. a chemical secreted by the adrenals
   _d_ signal   b. fluid emitted by a gland
   _a_ epinephrine c. a gland on top of the kidney
   _e_ nerves   d. a message
   _b_ secretion   e. carry signals between the body and the brain

Page 77

They Came from the North

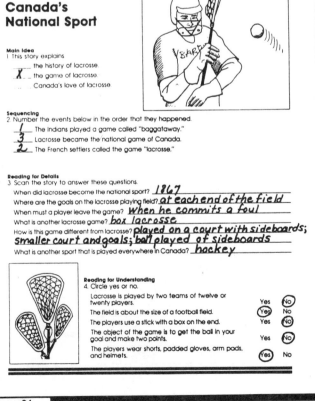

Main Idea
1. This story explains
   _____ how the Vikings were fierce warriors and pirates.
   __X__ how the Vikings influenced many cultures.
   _____ why the Vikings were not satisfied with their homeland.

Sequencing
2. Number the events below in the order that they happened.
   _3_ The Vikings began to move further west on their journeys.
   _2_ They raided towns and churches in search of gold.
   _1_ Vikings sailed away from their homes in search of riches.
   _5_ Many countries still show the influence of the Viking culture.
   _4_ Some of the Vikings began to settle in the countries they conquered.

Reading for Details
3. Scan the story to answer these questions.
   What countries were conquered by the Vikings? _England, Scotland, Ireland, Iceland, Greenland, Newfoundland, Russia, Turkey, Normandy_
   What were the Vikings looking for? _gold and riches_
   When did three Viking brothers found Gardarike? _874_
   Who adopted the Celtic custom of wearing the kilt and the tartan? _the vikings in Scotland_
   Why were the Vikings able to travel so easily? _They were close to the sea and became great sailors_

Reading for Understanding
4. Circle yes or no.
   The country I was born in was cold and bountiful.   Yes **No**
   I was a trader.   **Yes** No
   I traveled west to England, Scotland, and Iran.   Yes **No**
   Others that I knew went east into Russia and Turkey.   **Yes** No

Page 79

Canada's National Sport

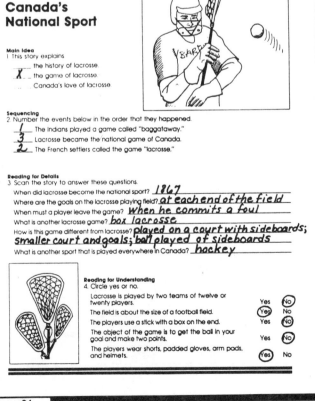

Main Idea
1. This story explains
   _____ the history of lacrosse.
   __X__ the game of lacrosse.
   _____ Canada's love of lacrosse.

Sequencing
2. Number the events below in the order that they happened.
   _1_ The Indians played a game called "baggataway."
   _3_ Lacrosse became the national game of Canada.
   _2_ The French settlers called the game "lacrosse."

Reading for Details
3. Scan the story to answer these questions.
   When did lacrosse become the national sport? _1867_
   Where are the goals on the lacrosse playing field? _at each end of the field_
   When must a player leave the game? _When he commits a foul_
   What is another lacrosse game? _box lacrosse_
   How is this game different from lacrosse? _played on a court with sideboards; smaller court and goals; ball played of sideboards_
   What is another sport that is played everywhere in Canada? _hockey_

Reading for Understanding
4. Circle yes or no.
   Lacrosse is played by two teams of twelve or twenty players.   Yes **No**
   The field is about the size of a football field.   **Yes** No
   The players use a stick with a box on the end.   Yes **No**
   The object of the game is to get the ball in your goal and make two points.   Yes **No**
   The players wear shorts, padded gloves, arm pads, and helmets.   **Yes** No

Page 81

Answer Key

Naming the Months

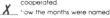

Main Idea

1. This story explains

____ why some months have 31 days.

____ how the Greeks and Romans cooperated.

X how the months were named.

Sequencing

2. Number the events below in the order that they happened.

1 Julius Caesar borrowed a calendar from the Greeks.

3 Julius Caesar named July after himself.

4 Augustus became Emperor.

2 Augustus made the calendar official.

Reading for Details

3. Scan the story to answer these questions.

Who was emperor when the Romans borrowed the Greek calendar? _Julius Caesar_

Where did the Romans get the names for their new calendar? _They kept the names from the Greek calendar._

When was the Greek calendar made official? _4 A.D._

What was the main difference between the Greek and Roman calendars? _the month that it started_

Why did both Julius Caesar and Augustus Caesar shorten February? _too add days to their own months_

Reading for Understanding

4. Place the correct letter in the blank.

c March   a. named for Julius Caesar

e May   b. means to cleanse

g June   c. named for the Roman god of war, Mars

a July   d. means seventh month

d September   e. named for the greek goddess, Maia

h October   f. means tenth month

i November   g. named for the Roman goddess, Juno

f December   h. means eighth month

b February   i. means ninth month

Page 83

The Domesday Book

Main Idea

1. This story explains

____ how William the Conqueror became King of England.

X how the Domesday Book came to be.

____ how people lived in the early days of England.

Sequencing

2. Number the events below in the order that they happened.

5 Information was recorded in the Domesday Book.

3 William the Conqueror demanded that everyone pay taxes to him.

4 William sent commissioners to each county to gather information.

1 William the Conqueror invaded England.

2 William the Conqueror became King of England.

Reading for Details

3. Scan the story to answer these questions.

Who came to England in 490 A.D.? _Angles and Saxons_

Where did they come from? _Germany_

What did they give to their war leaders? _loyalty and taxes_

When did William the Conqueror invade England? _1066_

Why did life change for the Anglo-Saxons? _William made them pay taxes to him instead of their war leaders._

Reading for Understanding

4. Circle yes or no.

I went to every country in Europe.   Yes **(No)**

I talked to the sheriff, the priest, a landowner, and six peasants.   **(Yes)** No

I asked how much the land was worth and how many houses were on it.   **(Yes)** No

I wrote everything down in the Domesday Book.   **(Yes)** No

I ended up with not only a tax record for the king, but a great history book.   **(Yes)** No

Page 85

The Story of Glass

Main Idea

1. This story explains

____ life without glass.

____ the material used in glassmaking.

X a short history of glass.

Sequencing

2. Number the events below in the order that they happen.

2 The materials are cooled.

1 Silica and other materials are melted together.

3 They form a cold, thick liquid.

4 Products are made from the glass.

Reading for Details

3. Scan the story to answer these questions.

When was glass as valuable as gold? _600 years ago_

What kind of glass is usually made today? _soda-lime._

Where did glassmakers first learn to swirl colors through their glass? _Venice, Italy_

Why is glass an important part of our lives? _It makes life easier and prettier._

Why does some glass change its shape over time? _because it is not solid_

Reading for Understanding

4. Place the word or phrase in the correct column.

Inexpensive, fine quality, very beautiful, made centuries ago, no two pieces are the same, used to make lenses for eyeglasses, used to make windows, used to make radio and TV tubes, popular today

Soda-lime Glass	Lead Glass	Venetian Glass
inexpensive; made centuries ago; used to make windows	_fine quality; used to make lenses for eye-glasses; used to make radio and TV tubes_	_very beautiful; no two pieces the same; popular today_

Page 87

The Knights of Japan

Main Idea

1. Choose another title for this story.

____ Born to be Warriors

____ How to Care for a Samurai Sword

X The Samurai

Sequencing

2. Number the events below in the order that they happened.

1 Boys were born into samurai families.

2 The boys entered training when they were still young.

3 Special teachers taught the boys skills needed to be a good samurai.

4 After training, the samurai promised to protect the nobleman and to fight for him.

5 In return, the nobleman gave many things to the samurai.

Reading for Details

3. Scan the story to answer these questions.

When did knights dress in armor? _600 years ago_

What were Japanese knights called? _samurai_

How did someone get to be a samurai? _only sons of samurai_

What things were part of a samurai training? _music, writing, art lessons_

Why did the samurai's sword maker say special prayers? _so the sword would be perfect_

Reading for Understanding

4. Circle yes or no.

Because I am the son of a samurai warrior, I am learning how to fight.   **(Yes)** No

I am also learning how to be a gentleman.   **(Yes)** No

I have to learn how to endure pain loudly.   Yes **(No)**

I must not be loyal, surrender, or shame a nobleman.   Yes **(No)**

My most important possession is my sword.   **(Yes)** No

Page 89

Poetry— The Rhythm of Words

Main Idea
1. The story explains
- __X__ how poetry got its rhythm
- _____ how poetry is different from music
- _____ the history of poetry.

Sequencing
2. Number the events below in the order that they happened.
- _1_ The songs and dances were prayers or magic spells.
- _4_ Bards would sing these stories from memory.
- _3_ The songs grew into long stories.
- _2_ People began to make songs for special occasions.
- _5_ Pure poetry was born when the songs were written down and became separate from the music.

Reading for Details
3. Scan the story to answer these questions.
- What is the most important feature of poetry? _its rhythm_
- How did poetry first get its rhythm? _from chanting to drums_
- What were most poems about at first? _heroes or adventures_
- When did the Greeks write down The Iliad and The Odyssey? _500 B.C._
- Why did people write poetry later? _for its beauty_

Reading for Understanding
4. Place the correct letter in the blank
- _b_ drums — a. long story-poems
- _c_ chants — b. instrument for beating out rhythm of dances
- _e_ bards — c. words that fit the rhythm of the drums
- _d_ Odysseus — d. Greek hero in two long songs
- _a_ epics — e. special performers who would sing long stories from memory

Page 91

Heroes and Messengers

Main Idea
1. Choose another title for this story.
- _____ By Pigeon or By Car
- _____ Pigeons in World War II
- __X__ The Talented Pigeon

Sequencing
2. Number the events below in the order that they happen.
- _4_ The owner puts the band in a special clock to record the finishing time.
- _1_ Each pigeon is taken an equal distance from its home.
- _5_ The clocks are taken to the racing club, and the times are recorded.
- _2_ The bird is released, and the starting time is written down.
- _3_ When the pigeon gets home, the owner takes the band off the pigeon's leg.

Reading for Details
3. Scan the story to answer these questions.
- What special ability does the pigeon have that makes it useful to humans? _homing — to find its way home from 100's of miles away_
- When were pigeons used for carrying messages? _in World War II_
- What is the most popular use of pigeons today? _racing_
- Where is pigeon racing especially popular? _Belgium_
- Why is a pigeon called a poor mans race horse? _because it doesn't cost alot to raise and race them_

Reading for Understanding
4. What is the topic of Paragraph 4?
- _____ winning races
- __X__ pigeon racing
- _____ timing the race

Page 93

The Story of the Harpsichord

Main Idea
1. Choose another title for this story.
- _____ The Piano Becomes King
- __X__ The Forerunner of the Piano
- _____ European Musical Instruments

Sequencing
2. Number the events below in the order that they happened.
- _3_ The spinet grew to the full-sized harpsichord.
- _4_ The harpsichord became a very popular instrument.
- _2_ The virginal gradually changed to the larger spinet.
- _1_ The harpsichord began as an instrument called a virginal.
- _5_ The piano replaced the harpsichord.

Reading for Details
3. Scan the story to answer these questions.
- Who were some of the great composers of the 16th-18th centuries? _Bach, Handel, Mozart_
- What instrument did they write music for? _harpsichord_
- When did people first play the harpsichord? _16th century_
- What was one of the harpsichord's faults? _could not vary sound_
- Why did the piano become more popular than the harpsichord? _because it could get louder or softer_

Reading for Understanding
4. Place the correct letter in the blank.
- _e_ virginal — a. Italian word meaning soft
- _c_ spinet — b. full name of the piano
- _b_ pianoforte — c. developed from the virginal
- _a_ piano — d. Italian word meaning loud
- _d_ forte — e. the earliest harpsichord

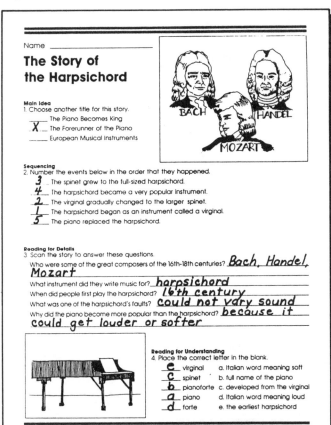

Page 95

The Golden People

Main Idea
1. Choose another title for this story.
- __X__ An Empire Remembered Today
- _____ The Art of the Aztecs
- _____ A History of Mexico

Sequencing
2. Number the events below in the order that they happened.
- _2_ Cortez and his troops came to Mexico.
- _3_ Cortez held Montezuma prisoner.
- _4_ The Aztecs fought against Cortez.
- _1_ The Aztecs settled in a valley in Mexico.
- _5_ Cortez conquered the Aztecs.

Reading for Details
3. Scan the story to answer these questions.
- Who lived in the Mexican valley before the Aztecs? _Toltecs_
- When did the Aztecs build their capital city? _167 years before Columbus sailed to America_
- What did the Aztec artists make? _earrings, necklaces, bracelets_
- What materials did they like to use? _gold, feathers, silver, jewels_
- How did the Aztecs show they were a peaceful people? _loved animals and flowers; gardens; fond of music, dancing, literature_
- Why did the Aztecs fight the Spanish? _to protect their civilization_

Reading for Understanding
4. Place the correct letter in the blank.
- _e_ Aztecs — a. used as altars by the Aztec priests
- _b_ Montezuma — b. aztec ruler
- _d_ Tenochtitlan — c. also astronomers who invented a complicated calendar
- _a_ Pyramids — d. great Aztec capital city
- _c_ Priests — e. a powerful Indian tribe in North America

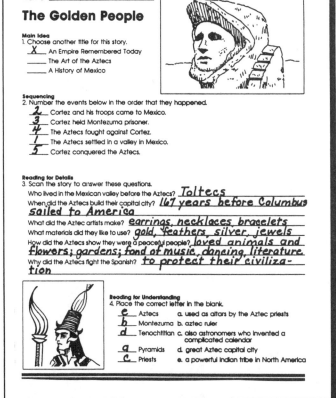

Page 97

Answer Key

An International Game

Main Idea
1. This story tells about
_____ the game of baseball.
_____ people who play cricket.
__X__ the game of cricket.

Sequencing
2. Number the events below in the order that they happened.
__4__ The countries became independent.
__1__ Shepherds in England used their staffs as bats.
__3__ The British people brought cricket to many countries.
__2__ Cricket gained popularity in England when rules were made.
__5__ The countries continued to play cricket.

Reading for Details
3. Scan the story to answer these questions.
Who has made cricket one of the world's most popular sports? _cricket lovers_

Where do cricket lovers live? _Jamaica, New Zealand, India, England_
When was cricket popular in the U.S. and Canada? _1800's_
What other game became popular during the Civil War? _baseball_
Why did this happen? _needs less room to play_

Reading for Understanding
4. Write "B" if the item describes only baseball. Write "C" if it describes only cricket. Write "both" if the item describes both cricket and baseball.
both Winner is the team who scores the most runs.
__C__ has a bowler
__b__ nine players on a team
both one team fields while the other team bats
__b__ has a pitcher
__C__ two batters at one time
__b__ nine innings
__b__ one batter at a time
__C__ two innings
__C__ eleven players on a team

Page 99

The Family of Words

Main Idea
1. This story tells about
__X__ the study of words.
_____ the changing meaning of words.
_____ words in the English language.

Sequencing
2. Number the events below in the order that they happened.
__1__ English started as the language of the Anglo-Saxons.
__5__ Pronunciation and spellings changed.
__2__ France invaded England.
__4__ Foreign words were used more often.
__3__ Many French words found their way into the English language.

Reading for Details
3. Scan the story to answer these questions.
Who are word detectives? _etymologists_
What do they do? _search through languages of many countries to find out where a word comes from_
Why have few of the foreign words in the English language stayed exactly the same? _gradually changed with use over time._
What did the word "salary" originally mean? _money given to Roman soldiers to buy salt_
What does the word "salary" mean now? _regular payment for doing a job_

Reading for Understanding
4. Place the correct letter in the blank.
__b__ Etymology a. comes from Latin and French
__c__ Coffee b. comes from Greek
__d__ Chocolate c. comes from Arabia
__e__ Tea d. comes from South American Indian word "cacahuatl"
__a__ Salary e. comes from ancient Chinese words "d'a" or "cha"

Page 101

Ancient Sign of Friendship

Main Idea
1. Choose another title for this story.
_____ Customs in Many Countries
_____ Knights in Armor
__X__ The Handshake and Other Signs of Friendliness

Sequencing
2. Number the sentences below in the order that you read about them.
__2__ Roman soldiers clasped each other's arms in greeting.
__5__ People in Japan or China may bow instead of shaking hands.
__4__ Knights in the Middle Ages clasped right hands.
__1__ Primitive people extended their empty hands to show they didn't wish to fight.
__3__ Arabs clasped hands so neither person would feel inferior.

Reading for Details
3. Scan the story to answer these questions.
Who may have begun the practice of clasping right hands? _the Greeks_

Where does a person sometimes touch his fingertips together to show respect? _In India_

Who raises one arm in greeting a friend? _some African people_
How do some Europeans greet each other? _kissing each other's cheeks_

Reading for Understanding
4. Why did these people shake hands? Place the correct letter in the blank.
__d__ Primitive traveler a. to show respect by kissing a superior person's hand
__b__ Roman soldier b. had a special greeting only he could use
__a__ Arabs c. to make sure that each could not draw his sword
__c__ Knights d. to show that he had no weapons

Page 103

A New Way of Life

Main Idea
1. Choose another title for this story.
_____ A New Governor
_____ Louisiana Settlers
__X__ The Cajuns

Sequencing
2. Number the events below in the order that they happened.
__4__ The Acadians were forced to leave Acadia.
__2__ The British defeated the French.
__1__ French people farmed the valleys of Acadia.
__3__ Acadia came under British control.
__5__ The Acadians moved to Louisiana.

Reading for Details
3. Scan the story to answer these questions.
What modern-day provinces made up Acadia? _Nova Scotia and part of New Brunswick in Canada_
When did French Acadia come under British control? _1755_

Why were the Acadians sent to Louisiana? _to make way for British settlers; It was a French colony._
What did the Acadians do in Louisiana instead of farming? _fishing and trapping muskrats_
Who are the Cajuns? _descendents of the French Acadians_
What are the Cajuns especially known for? _their cooking_

Reading for Understanding
4. Place the correct letter in the blank.
__d__ bayous a. wall built to keep out water
__c__ flax b. a narrow boat
__a__ dike c. spun to make linen
__b__ pirogue d. slow, steamy rivers
__e__ Cajuns e. new name of Acadians

Page 105

Myths, Legends, Neat Things IF8714

126

© 1990 Instructional Fair, Inc.

The Big Sound

Main Idea
1. Choose another title for this story.
___ Sounding Together
_X_ The Symphony Orchestra
___ How Painters and Composers are Alike

Sequencing
2. Number these sentences in the order you read about them.
_2_ The woodwinds add color to the sound.
_5_ All instruments play together.
_4_ Percussion instruments add special effects.
_1_ The strings set the mood of the piece.
_3_ The brass instruments give the orchestra life.

Reading for Details
3. Scan the story to answer these questions.
Who writes the music for a symphony orchestra? _a composer_
What is the largest and most important group in a symphony? _the strings_
Which instruments make flowing, sweet sounds? _woodwind_
What is the purpose of a symphony orchestra? _to create music_
How many instruments are usually in the symphony orchestra? (Do not include the extra percussion instruments.) _98_

Reading for Understanding
4. Place each of these instruments in the correct column.

violins, French horns, drums, flutes, violas, trumpet, bells, oboes, cellos, trombones, chimes, clarinets, basses, bassoons, harp, tuba

Woodwinds	Strings	Brass	Percussion
flutes	violins	Fr. horns	drums
oboes	violas	trumpet	bells
clarinets	cellos	trombones	chimes
bassoons	basses	tuba	
	harp		

Page 107

The Wall the Romans Built

Main Idea
1. Choose another title for this story.
_X_ The Story of Hadrian's Wall
___ The Invasion of Britain
___ The Fighting Picts

Sequencing
2. Number the events below in the order that they happened.
_5_ Roman soldiers manned the forts along the wall.
_1_ The Romans invaded Britain.
_4_ Hadrian's Wall was built.
_3_ The Picts attacked the Romans.
_2_ The Picts refused to be conquered.
_6_ The Roman soldiers left Britain.

Reading for Details
3. Scan the story to answer these questions.
When did the Romans invade Britain? _43 A.D._
Who accepted the Roman's rule quickly? _Celts_
Where did the Picts live? _far to the north in the rugged hills_
Why did Hadrian order a wall built? _to keep the Picts away_
Why were there ditches along the wall? _to help keep the Picts away_

Reading for Understanding
4. Circle yes or no.
Hadrian's wall took seventeen years to build. Yes / **No**
It was 11 kilometers or 74 miles long. **Yes** / No
It was 8 feet or 2.5 meters thick. **Yes** / No
No one needed to take care of the wall. Yes / **No**
In 383 the wall was abandoned. **Yes** / No

Page 109

Curds and Whey

Main Idea
1. This story tells about
_X_ making cheese.
___ the ingredients in cheese.
___ different kinds of cheese.

Sequencing
2. Number the events below in the order that they happened.
_3_ The whey is poured off.
_1_ Bacteria are added to the milk.
_4_ The curd is cut into pieces and pressed into a mold.
_2_ Rennet is added to the milk.
_5_ When the cheese is solid and dry, it is taken out of the mold.
_6_ The cheese is wrapped and left to age.

Reading for Details
3. Scan the story to answer these questions.
Who had a lucky accident? _Arab lad_
What did he put into his bag? _milk_
When did he find a lump of cheese? _when he opened the bag_
What is added to milk to turn it into cheese? _bacteria_

Why do most people eat cheese? _They love the taste._

Reading for Understanding
4. Place the correct letter in the blank.
_b_ bacteria   a. the watery liquid left when milk separates
_d_ aging   b. give cheese different flavors
_a_ whey   c. a digestive juice produced by sheep and cattle
_c_ rennet   d. helps improve the flavor of cheese
_e_ curd   e. solid part left when milk separates

Page 111

Surveying— Mapmaking and More

Main Idea
1. This story explains
___ using surveys for construction.
_X_ different reasons for making surveys.
___ how maps are made.

Sequencing
2. Number the events below in the order that they happen.
_2_ Surveyors go out to the proposed site.
_4_ Surveyors make two kinds of drawings.
_1_ Someone wants to build a road, building, or railway.
_3_ Surveyors take measurements of the land.
_6_ Construction can begin.
_5_ Surveyors go back into the field and lay out the project.

Reading for Details
3. Scan the story to answer these questions.
When do you see the result of surveying? _when you look at maps_
What are some services performed by surveyors? _determining property lines; surveys for buildings, railroads, roads_
What two measurements are needed to build a road? _ups and downs of the land and distances_
Why do surveyors measure the size of a lake? _to know how much water is in it_
Why do they map out the bottom of a lake? _to find dangerous shallow places_

Reading for Understanding
4. Place the correct letter in the blank.
_c_ elevation   a. exact; definite; accurate
_d_ "lay out"   b. art and science of measuring the land
_b_ surveying   c. drawing that shows how much earth must be removed or added before construction begins
_e_ property lines d. procedure where a project is precisely measured and marked with wooden stakes
_a_ precision   e. used so people know who owns a piece of land

Page 113